W9-BIY-190

Technologies
of Knowing

Also by John Willinsky

....

Learning to Divide the World
Education at Empire's End

Empire of Words
The Reign of the OED

The Triumph of Literature / The Fate of Literacy

The New Literacy
Redefining Reading and Writing
in the Schools

The Well-Tempered Tongue
The Politics of Standard English
in High School

Technologies of Knowing

....

*A Proposal for
the Human Sciences*

....

John Willinsky

Beacon Press

BOSTON

Beacon Press
25 Beacon Street, Boston, Massachusetts 02108-2892
www.beacon.org

Beacon Press books are published under the auspices
of the Unitarian Universalist Association of Congregations.

Cartoon on page 3 © Jim Borgman.
Reprinted with permission of King Features Syndicate.

03 02 01 00 99   8 7 6 5 4 3 2 1

This book is printed on recycled acid-free paper that contains at least
20 percent postconsumer waste and meets the uncoated paper
ANSI/NISO specifications for permanence as revised in 1992.

Text design by Boskydell Studio
Composition by Wilsted & Taylor Publishing Services

Library of Congress Cataloging-in-Publication Data
Willinsky, John, 1950–
Technologies of knowing : a proposal for the
social sciences / John Willinsky.
p.   cm.
Includes bibliographical references and index.
ISBN 0-8070-6106-9 (cloth)
1. Communication in the social sciences.   I. Title.
H61.8.W55   1999
302—dc21   98-39526

To V. L. F.

Contents

1

....

Random News

I T SEEMS APT to begin a book on the strained relationship between social science research and the public with an editorial
cartoon that takes a jab at what the public has learned to expect from research. The heading on Jim Borgman's cartoon in
the *Cincinnati Enquirer* gives it away: "Today's Random Medical
News, from the *New England Journal of Panic-Inducing Gobbledy-
gook.*"[1] So much research, so much random news. We no longer
expect entirely consistent or particularly coherent information
on what affects us across a whole range of issues in our lives, from
our family's health to its education. Where research on social issues does not breed public indifference, it induces a crisis of confidence of the sort Borgman is playing on.

But then the headlines of the typical Health News column in
the paper actually do have a Ripley's-Believe-It-or-Not quality
to them on any given week: "Death Not Stalking Lefties," "ASA
Starves Colon Cancer," "Asbestos, Cancer Link Studied," and
"Let There Be Light in Nurseries."[2] All of it true and all of it
mildly fascinating over breakfast, but these little info-bites only

add to the general sense of being awash in a world of well-funded research, sinking in a sea of churning information.

At first glance, this may just seem a public relations problem for the research industry. And that has been the response of some working within the universities, who have concluded that their institution simply needs to do a better job of getting the word out on the value of their research programs and accomplishments. For example, at the University of British Columbia, where I work, the lampposts have recently begun sporting colorful banners with the slogan "Think About It: UBC Research." One wonders if those behind this campaign were oblivious to the danger that thinking about it might well draw attention to the very crisis of confidence and indifference Borgman is addressing, the very issue that forms the topic of this book. For in a sense, I too am asking that we *think about it*: think about the public return on the vast amount of research that has been conducted and is currently underway; think about whether the research community is doing enough to ensure that the fruits of its labors really stand as a public resource and good. And while this sense of public trust applies to all that the universities do in the name of research, I think it has a special poignancy when it comes to the social sciences, which are working on issues that might be said to fall more fully than other academic disciplines within the interests of *public knowledge*. Put simply, this book is about whether more can be done to bring social science research within the scope of public knowledge.

Certainly, judging from newspaper coverage, people's interests in research extend beyond the social sciences, with their focus on health, education, justice, and welfare. However, those who are interested in whether the expansion of the universe is indefinite

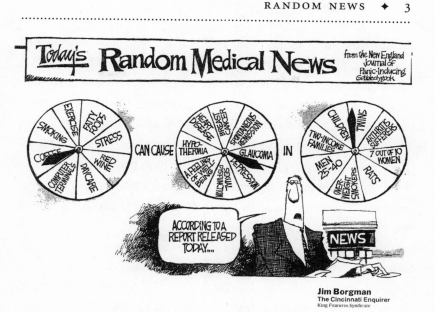

Jim Borgman
The Cincinnati Enquirer
King Features Syndicate

rather than cyclical seldom despair over the progress being made in astronomy. Those who are curious about whether the genome project will result in better treatments for a range of diseases expect slow and steady progress in unraveling this complex code. What the public is less patient with, what raises the ire of editorial cartoonists and editorial writers, is the inability of research to be more decisively helpful on that whole range of human activities that have been the subject of systematic research for well over a century. With the social sciences, there is the longstanding promise of a knowledge to which people should be able to turn freely for guidance. There is the hope that they can find greater satisfaction in life, secure greater justice for themselves and others. There is the aspiration to better understand how we are to live together, to better understand the sense of it all.

The social sciences typically comprise the academic disciplines of anthropology, economics, political science, psychology, and sociology, as well as the professional schools of education, social work, business, and health sciences. Research in these areas deploys a wide range of techniques, including statistics, surveys, interviews, the analysis of documents, and ethnographic descriptions of how people live. This research leads to models and theories of how people act, and it influences programs and policies. It is knowledge concerned with how we are governed and educated, how we work and play, how we live and understand that life.

Given that this broad body of knowledge may have more to offer the public than is currently being realized, I am proposing that the great intellectual challenge of this Age of Information is not coming up with a grand unified theory in physics, or discovering the origins of human life. The great challenge is to be better served by what we already *know*. How can the public be better served by the knowledge assembled on its behalf? Here we are living in a *knowledge economy*, while the particular body of knowledge assembled by the social sciences, devoted as these fields are to improving the condition of humankind, is kept virtually out of general circulation? Here we have this computer revolution networking the world, and the social sciences cannot find the means or will to establish technologies of knowing that would enable its potential contribution to this knowledge economy to flow freely among the public, that it might irrigate democratic debate and processes.

In the meantime, the corporate world is scrambling to manage, package, and commercialize knowledge to service a wider public. Knowledge is spoken of as power and product, while it is turned by new technologies into the dynamo driving innovation, marketing, and client satisfaction. It may once have been that knowledge was to universities what automobiles were to industry. It is no longer. Knowledge is commodity and economy within the private sector. And I feel that this calls for a revitalization of knowledge's place within the public sector. For if the universities are to continue to receive public support in their ostensible pursuit of knowledge as a free and public good, it may no longer be sufficient to continue that ancient habit of shelving the resulting knowledge in campus libraries, on the off chance that especially keen segments of the public will come looking for it.

In an effort to redress the imbalance between private and public knowledge sectors, I am proposing that the social sciences explore new ways of increasing their knowledgeable contribution to the public sector. This is only to move the particular knowledge economy of the social sciences into far more general circulation. It calls for the social sciences to better attune themselves to those they aspire to serve. It is to recognize that the public status of knowledge has changed in the latter years of this millennium, changed in ways that the social sciences have not kept up with. It is to ask whether the social sciences could make better use of technology, in its original sense of techné, as an art and craft, to bring greater coherence and coordination to the research enterprise, to render it more broadly intelligible in its limits and variety of approaches, while improving public access to what is supposed to be, after all, a public good.

Simply stated, I believe that social science research can be and must be made more helpful to more people. In particular, the social sciences can contribute far more to forms of public knowledge that not only help us to understand different aspects of the world, but (with some care) can do so in a way that expands the reach of democracy. The alternative? The social sciences continue producing knowledge that induces a sense of public indifference punctuated by moments of exasperation.

One of those moments is taking place, for example, with the current state of confusion over the detection of breast cancer. Research has failed to ascertain whether mammograms for middle-aged women and breast self-examination more generally are a good idea or not. This is not for want of research, although there is clearly more to be done. Nor is medical science at issue. The problem is with the science research that tracks what happens to large groups of women who do and do not undertake these procedures.

The current state of this research has led the American Cancer Society to say "yes" to annual mammograms. The U.S. National Cancer Institute has gone back and forth on the issue. And the Canadian Cancer Society finds the evidence does not warrant having a mammogram. The ever-present *New England Journal of Medicine*, after reviewing the research, said it is a "toss-up" between doing nothing and having an X-ray. Only after the age of fifty are the mammogram's advantages in detecting the mortality rate of the disease unequivocal.[3]

A similar lack of resolve in the research has led increasing numbers of doctors to stop recommending breast self-examination. The "lukewarm" research findings, as the *New York Times* put it, are not thought to warrant the psychological burden of searching for this deadly disease on a monthly basis.[4] The United States Preventive Services Task Force has gone a step further with its declaration that there is "insufficient evidence to recommend either for or against breast self-examination."[5] These various societies and task forces feel it is their job to declare in favor of or against these practices, and this is not proving helpful. They appear convinced that the public could not handle the far more subtle and tentative forms of knowledge produced by this research.[6]

On the other hand, I believe that adequate summaries of the research that convey the relative effectiveness of self-examinations and mammograms at a certain age should be made readily available. Those summaries could make apparent those points at which contradictions abound or where there is insufficient evidence. Certainly, much more could be done to ensure that the data collected can be compared and combined. In this book I explore ways of increasing the compatibility of existing research programs, while expanding the range of inquiry open to public scrutiny.

The reaction among women to the ineptitude surrounding the research and treatment of breast cancer has grown from anger into activism focused on, among other things, the right to information. We are witnessing how this info age can breed *info-rage*. It is fostering a sense of information interests and rights among the public. The "surging breast-cancer movement," as the newspaper names it, has generated massive conferences of breast-cancer survivors; it has spurred environmentalists to study the role of toxins in the disease; and it has drawn researchers to examine alternative medicine.[7]

On a broader medical scale, this public interest in knowledge has led to an online version of the National Library of Medicine (NLM), which offers a compendium of nine million references and 4,000 medical journal abstracts. Launched in June 1997, the NLM's website at this writing receives some 50,000 "visits" a day.[8] "Consumers don't want just a general overview of a particular diagnosis or a particular treatment," observes William Reece, the founder of HealthGate Data Corporation, which conducts research for doctors and patients, "What we're finding is that they are really drilling down into clinical articles that, three years ago, only a physician would have read."[9] The feminist movement certainly deserves credit for this shift from relying on professionals' opinions to finding out for ourselves. The turning point in this process may well have been the publication in 1973 of the manifesto *Our Bodies, Ourselves*, by the Boston Women's Health Book Collective.[10]

Yet how much farther ahead have we come in what we know of ourselves since then? And why is it that what we know is so often at odds with what we knew last year, so un-reassuring, at a time when we are otherwise wired into an Age of Information? How can the enormous public and private investment in research generate this dual impression of both information explosion and exasperation? If "civilization is an enormous device for economizing on knowledge," as Stanford social scientist Thomas Sowell has put it, one has also to wonder just how civilized we are, amid the seeming haphazardness and incoherence that exists within the social science sector of this oft-proclaimed knowledge economy.[11]

A number of tightly contained information systems have been perfected. As a result, the U.S. government can place a remote-controlled wagon on Mars and, for that matter, manufacturers can turn out mildew-resistant shower curtains that work. Yet across a broad front of human activities, social science research fails to inspire public confidence in what it has determined about bilingual education, reading instruction, welfare reform, intelligence assessment, and the status of the family, to name issues this book will visit. The problem is not a lack of interest in knowing, as the breast-cancer movement and National Library of Medicine examples illustrate. As it stands, the dedication and talent devoted to social science research is largely lost to the public, as well as to practitioners in such related professions as medicine, education, and social services. But then I will also argue that the quality of this knowledge would also benefit from the vitality and dynamics of the greater public engagement I am proposing.

As things now stand, professors of this and that are regular pop-up features on the evening news, part of the sound-bite info-economy of the mass media, where a lifetime of research and inquiry is reduced to a couple of sentences in the studio, often interrupted by a dissenting colleague from across the continent. A few write for the op-ed pages and the serious press. But that great body of academic inquiry largely marches off into the indexed obscurity of academic journaldom, perhaps where most of it belongs, but perhaps not.

I do not want to deny that research studies have helped governments to form policy, and citizens' groups to fight that policy. They have guided doctors' advice to patients and schoolteachers' selection of reading programs. Studies have helped union leaders to organize employees, and big corporations to devise minority recruitment strategies. Yet if the entirety of social science research is publicly available, often for no more than the price of university library parking, there is no getting around how difficult it is to navigate, find, sort out, and reconcile. It would seem to require its own Freedom of Information Act, in which freedom would amount not just to reasonable access but to freedom from incomprehensibility.

My proposal for improving public access and intelligibility is to lay out in these pages the makings of a whimsical corporate enterprise dedicated to turning social science research into public knowledge. The fictional company is intended to provoke and focus the debate over the relationship between the social sciences and the public. The idea for the company grows out of my work as a professor of education who conducts social science research on teaching and learning. You might say that when it comes to the public value of this research, I am either part of the problem or part of the solution, to recall the challenge the late Eldridge Cleaver threw at my generation some years ago. With this book, I step back from more typical educational studies to consider one possible solution.

Perhaps it would have been wiser to mind the quality of my own work rather than seeking to disturb the well-oiled machinery of the profession with such fantastical proposals. Writing about the near-future prospects of knowledge in an age of information technologies is not, as we say in scholarly circles, my area. My scant but not improbable preparation for this work includes studies of earlier knowledge systems, such as the *Oxford English Dictionary,* that "great engine of research" as the Victorians called it, and imperialism's global research apparatus of expedition, exhibition, and education.[12] The difference between these knowledge systems and the project I am presenting here could be summed up as *that was then and this is not-yet.* The empire of the future may well be the empire of the mind, as Winston Churchill observed while the sun was setting on the British Empire. But that mind will be networked and data-based, as it stands poised to participate in the tele-imperium of the next millennium. How we, who research the social world, can ensure that a greater part of our contribution to that mind falls within the scale of democratic and public knowledge is the subject of this inquiry and proposal.

Both the problems and solutions to our knowledge troubles are bound to involve information technologies. Those of us in the research trade have been using computers for some years now to speed up and ease up—that is, to *automate*—what it takes to produce knowledge in our respective fields. We use these machines to gather, store, sort, calculate, analyze, write, circulate, present, and archive information, with an efficiency that might be accused of accelerating information glut. The machines extend the researcher's reach (assuming we are not simply extending the machine's reach) by expanding our professional contacts within the research community, as well as enabling us to create more of the same, more quickly and at greater expense. The social sciences are not yet using the technologies to assist the public in taking advantage of this body of publicly sponsored research.

In what follows, I am pushing for a possible history of knowledge's near future through a corporation for public knowledge that amounts to a social science fiction.[13] It is intended to ensure that we do not go gentle into that good night of information technologies and professional expertise that might only serve to diminish public knowledge and democratic participation.

Although I am turning to new information technologies to see throughg this corporate vision, I ask that you not mistake the machines for the point of this inquiry. They are only the provocation. They are incontournable, in the French sense of an impediment one cannot avoid or circumvent, in the knowledge trade today.[14] The machines serve as both metaphor and mechanical force. If, as literary critic I. A. Richards realized long before the computer, a book is a machine to think with, then what we have made of our machines is a way of thinking about what we want of the world, whether in our recreational vehicles or through a World Wide Web.

The technologies I deploy here are so minimally futuristic that I can use the present tense in writing about them. They exist in the here and now, and are not in the least anthropomorphic or human-like. They do not require the soft-spoken Artificial Intelligence of HAL or the charmingly mechanical busybodiness of C3PO, let alone the deadly cyborgism of the Terminator.

This effort to expand the social sciences' contribution to public knowledge is not about putting our faith in machines that, by virtue of network and database, will come up with the grand answers that currently allude us. It is only about asking whether there might be some way of testing and extending the public value of the knowledge the social sciences continue to accumulate in the belief that this knowledge can make a difference in the knowing. It all begins by imagining the social sciences working through a fictional corporation in the public interest.

2

....

Corporate Prospects

A T THE CENTER of this thought experiment on the near future of public knowledge stands the favored protagonist of cyberpunk fiction—the data-trafficking corporation. The method of this social science fiction is to demonstrate both the epistemological and the business purpose of a public corporation that would assume responsibility for bringing greater coherence and coordination, intelligibility and access, to the research and scholarship traditionally associated with the social sciences. Such would be the mission of . . . well, let me call it the Automata Data Corporation. The name seems to have just the right assonance to prevent anyone from taking it too seriously, for the goal here is not to promote the corporation but the prospects of reforming how the social sciences go about their knowledge business.

In the chapters that follow I address the challenges the social sciences face, using Automata Data as a foil, allowing me to suggest an alternative manner of directing research efforts in light of those challenges. As these challenges range from information excess to democratic uses of knowledge, I develop different aspects of what would be required of an Automata Data. This method can make it difficult to imagine what this corporation is all about.

Thus, at the outset, I want to offer a brief run-through of what I have made of Automata Data in an effort to take advantage of new information technologies and a reawakened determination within the social sciences on behalf of the public sector of this knowledge economy. Obviously, a corporation for public knowledge such as Automata Data is not going to be shaped by the vision of any one person, and so what follows is only an example or starting point for supporting the change I think we need to consider for the social sciences.

I am assuming that Automata Data would operate as a virtual corporation, with an electronic presence on the web that covered its full range of activity, from data sharing to research directories. Although it would commission studies and conduct its own program of research, it would principally network and index resources rather than own or publish them, providing guides and supports for utilizing those resources whether they be sources of raw data or the continually updated results of ongoing research programs. It would continue peer-review methods of maintaining a standard for what falls within the scope of the social science research and scholarship it presents.

As I have imagined it, Automata Data would need to serve three constituencies: those who fund social science research, those who conduct it, and those among the public and the media, as well as practitioners in many related professions, who would potentially use the accumulated knowledge.

For foundations, organizations, and government agencies that fund social science research, Automata Data Corporation would serve as a source of information, coordination, and commissioned research:

1. The Corporation would offer funding bodies a multidimensional mapping of research on a given topic, representing the links among the studies as well as the extent and nature of the research coverage. It would also provide a public-professional forum for discussing the research coverage on that topic, all of which could serve as one source of information in setting the funding agendas for such bodies.

2. Automata Data would also provide a research coordinating and brokering service that would enable funding and grant agencies to establish closely linked programs of research on a global basis across different populations, geographical areas, and over extended periods of time.

3. Finally, Automata Data would accept commissions to undertake programs of social science research for a variety of agencies, while ensuring that the results of that work contribute to the public record.

For researchers, Automata Data could provide a starting point for planning research, or a final point of connection with other existing and ongoing work through the corporation's public-access web site:

1. Researchers would have the option of working directly through Automata Data from the very outset of their work or waiting until their project is finished and published, and then allowing Automata Data to either mount it on the corporate site or create hyperlinks to the study, and possibly to the data and instruments. Of course, researchers could also refuse to have any connection with Automata Data, in which case the Corporation could at best reference the work within its mapping of the research on a given topic.

2. In the planning stages of their work, researchers would turn to Automata Data for its brokering and networking of research contracts, collaborations, and other opportunities on a global basis and for its mapping of the research on a given topic by geography, populations, chronology, and research methods.

3. By using Automata Data to gain ready access to the components of research design of completed, current, and proposed studies within the corporation's network of research databases, researchers would be able to improve the integration of their research into the larger field of inquiry, enhancing the overall coherence of the resulting knowledge. Researchers would also have access to existing research data, as well as to government and commercial sources of data for which ongoing research access has been secured, with various modes of analysis already under way through the automated systems of the Corporation.

4. Researchers would be invited by Automata Data, in its research coordinating role, to address a broad range of empirical and theoretical issues that point to gaps and inadequacies in the analysis and coverage offered by the social sciences, working with scholars using more innovative methodologies as well as those conducting empirical research in the classic model of the statistical study. Researchers could expect their work on a topic to be layered within historical investigations, contemporary empirical studies, and conceptual inquiries, providing bridging pieces while inviting contributing researchers to discuss the connections. The Corporation would support the linking and integrating of a variety of research methods from statistical to narrative, with an aim to having this work do more than it might otherwise in speaking to the points of connection and contradiction within the scope of the knowledge the social sciences have to offer on a given topic.

For the public, media, and practitioners, Automata Data would provide carefully designed access to what the social sciences have to offer on a wide range of topics, as well as an opportunity to participate in that research:

1. Through Automata Data's web site, the public could search for the current state of social science research on a given topic, generating maps of linked studies along dimensions of geography, populations, chronology, and research methods. They would be able to skim among the standardized abstracts, pause over an article, or drill down to the data, whether in the form of statistics, sound recordings of interviews, or video clips. Their reading of the research would be suppported by various overviews, explanatory footnotes, and help screens provided by Automata Data to increase the intelligibility and coherence of the research presented.

2. The public's access to the data, information, and knowledge produced by the social sciences on a given topic would not be accompanied by recommendations from Automata Data on what to do, what policies should be followed, what programs are most likely to succeed, and so on. While striving to improve the coherence and coordination among studies is bound to entail value judgments, which will be open to ongoing critique and revision, Automata Data will remain committed to representing the diversity of knowledge and the contest of ideas within the social sciences.

3. The public would be able to volunteer to participate in proposed and current research and to donate encrypted and anonymous forms of the data associated with them in government and commercial databases, as well as to trace the results of research projects using that data. They would be able to join or initiate electronic forums with researchers and funding bodies discussing the social science research agenda.

It is fair to ask at the outset how such an unlikely contraption as a public corporation could ever hope to take on such an unwieldy mission as organizing the research activities of a vast array of autonomous social scientists. And my initial response is to ask in return that the practicality of the whole enterprise *not* be the sole measure by which this conjectured corporation be judged; suspend disbelief over the enormity of the whole of it and consider what its various strategies have to offer. My second response is to ask what it means not to do something about the degree of disarray within a field of research that is intended to be a public good.

As it turns out, this seemingly naïve hope to advance the public good through such a suspect vehicle as a corporation has its historical precedents. In the last century, schools and colleges all sought charters of incorporation, as did charitable societies and public utilities. They were seeking a measure of legal status within a defined purpose, limiting their liability to that purpose, while undertaking a convenience or necessity for the public.[1] Automata Data would be, in effect, a public utility for brokering data and coordinating research on behalf of individuals, interest groups, government agencies, and commercial enterprises. This act of incorporation would, among other things, make the knowledge produced by Automata Data susceptible to modern liability laws while ensuring that it kept to its purpose of improving public access to and intelligibility of that knowledge. It would be subject to consumer and bystander damage suits that might add a salutary note to work in the social sciences that has not otherwise been present.

One need not go far to find models of corporations in the public interest. The Corporation for Public Broadcasting is one obvious inspiration for this project. It operates the Public Broadcasting Service, with its radio companion, National Public Radio (NPR). For three decades now these networks have developed programming and supported local broadcasting stations, with public broadcasting ranking second to national defense in a Roper Starch Worldwide poll on the best value Americans received on their tax dollar.[2]

In the field of research, the federally chartered, private and nonprofit, National Academy of Sciences offers another model, with the "social and political sciences" among its twenty-five scientific sections. The government commissions the Academy (examples to follow) to review the state of research in areas of public concern, such as immigration, bilingualism, and literacy.[3] Or, more modestly in scope, Automata Data could follow the model of the Social Science Research Council, which according to its current president has "for nearly 75 years ... been a bridge-builder among universities, foundations, the disciplines and area studies associations, and government."[4] Automata Data could also turn to the Educational Testing Service (ETS), as a model of a successful public service corporation in the knowledge business.[5] It could also learn much from an organization such as Public Agenda, which identifies itself "as a private, nonpartisan, nonprofit public opinion research and citizen education organization" funded by foundations and trusts. It could borrow aspects of the think-tank model of the RAND Corporation, or the private research enterprise of Mathematica Policy Research, Inc.[6]

While I imagine Automata Data offering something more than each of these examples, I do not imagine everyone in the social sciences embracing its centralizing and coordinating interests, even as it strives for fairness in representing divergences and conflicts among research strands. Automata Data would itself represent a social experiment specifically directed at helping those concerned that their research efforts are not doing all that they could for more people, those who are willing to consider how such an incorporation of public, professional, and academic interests might improve the quality of public knowledge. It is intended to be a way of thinking through the ethical responsibilities of social science research, while testing and extending the role this knowledge might play in political and social processes.

A major aspect of Automata Data Corporation's elaborate experiment would be in exploring different ways of organizing and presenting the research in its public web site, permitting users to gain a sense of the different approaches taken by social scientists. It would, at the very least, enable users to pursue a topic by scanning abstracts linked to articles where one could compare results, examine data, and pose queries. There would be nothing so new in this organization, except for the steps it would take to support public use through additional notes, links, and concern with the overall intelligibility from the data to the topic level. It would allow one to focus on research that relates to one's own situation, or one could work back through the great chain of references, with support for grasping the relationship among various studies. Readers would have the resources at their fingertips, a mouse-click away, to compare the results from related studies, consult explanatory notes on research methods, and seek out studies on specific populations, while registering concerns in an online forum about the major gaps and unasked questions of a particular study.

This may seem an all-too-pedantic vision of the public's possible interest in this knowledge, and while there will only be limited circumstances in which the public wants to get to the bottom of these ideas, it seems their right and the social sciences' responsibility to make this possible, as if the inquiry really were all about expanding the possibilities of public knowledge.

All of this can be done today by walking into a good research library, although one needs to be equipped with the skills and stamina of a graduate student. The difference offered by Automata Data would be primarily a matter of degree, with greater ease of access supported by the dynamic generation of indexes and guides to the literature that could be driven by the user's interests, as well as by the very style of research that would be designed with this public purpose in mind. In addition to the studies themselves, the web site could utilize reviews and commentaries that deal with conflicting results and controversies, as well as setting up dialogues among researchers on what keeps them on different paths.

I see the impact of the Automata Data public access web site working in both directions. Public discourse, whether in the media or in open forums, should begin to reflect this greater access to what the social sciences have to offer. And the use of the site by those outside the profession, and the degree to which they use it, will have its own effect on the direction and style of the social sciences. At this point, research can seem to operate with little enough regard for how the results will be taken up by public interests. I recognize that the time, energy, and expense devoted to improving the design and presentation of research for its new public role would take resources that would otherwise have supported further studies. But this reduction in the sheer number of studies would not be a bad thing in itself.

Automata Data would have to make clear, as part of this dynamic web site, that what it was presenting reflected the state of its knowledge up to the moment of inquiry, with all of the variety, tentativeness, and degrees of uncertainty and probability that goes along with it. This information would be carefully presented to serve and inspire public debate, rather than bring such debate to an end through the authoritative declarations of an overconfident science.

Automata Data would undertake commissioned studies on behalf of private and government clients, individuals and advocacy groups, media services and public bodies. It would, of course, have to compete against many private agencies for such commissions, using to advantage its public commitments and talents at coordinating research. In its efforts to ensure that it contributes to, rather than diminishes, public participation in democratic processes through access to social science research, Automata Data would offer *pro bono* services to ensure equal access to its ability to conduct research and contribute to public debate. This, too, would form part of the ongoing experiment in assessing what these forms of knowledge bring to democratic processes. As such, Automata Data is but a way of ensuring that the data-intensive cyberspace that encircles the globe, forming perhaps our hope for an ozone substitute, has within it an alternative politics of knowledge to the one that tends to dominate transnational capitalism.[7]

Before coming up with this public corporate model for Automata Data, I did consider using a Quaker-ish Society of Friends of Knowledge, until I realized that in many respects this is what we already have in the form of the various professional associations for social scientists. These helpful organizations, with their profusion of journals and conferences directed at serving the professional needs of their members, actually end up forming part of the argument in favor of an alternative coordinating agency such as Automata Data that would take on serving public interests as its primary function. Still, I cannot shake the feeling that it is plain reckless to conjure up such a Faustian incorporation in the name of knowledge. Oscar Wilde warned that having one's dreams come true was much the worst of the two possibilities for dreams. Perhaps my consolation with the Automata Data scenario laid out here is that it is bound to leave plenty of room for cyberpunk data disruption, Greenpeace-style protest action, and other such checks on any one entity's power to own the know.

Although I have made much of the fictional nature of this corporate conjuring, I should also point out, without presuming comparison, that Francis Bacon is said to have launched the Royal Society, the oldest and among the most significant scientific organizations in the English-speaking world, through the suggestiveness of his posthumously published science fiction. *The New Atlantis* was a fable, his editor explained in 1627, one Bacon had intended to encourage "great and marvelous works for the benefit of men" by laying out a vision that, if too ambitious in parts, "most things therein are within men's powers to effect."[8] The far-off and lost world of Solomon's House (or the College of the Six Days' Work) was staffed by Merchants of Light, Depredators, Mystery-men, and Pioneers. Their job was to scour the world, each gathering different sorts of books, abstracts, and experiments, which they turned over to the Compilers, who drew "the experiments of the former four into titles and tables, to give better light for the drawing of observations and axioms out of them," and the Benefactors, who "cast about how to draw out of them things of use and practice for man's life and knowledge."[9]

Bacon's *New Atlantis* bore the subtitle *Work Unfinished*, and it is as wise a disclaimer as I can imagine for any utopian vision. There are those today who still hope to see Bacon's dream realized, not least of all advocates of the "emerging entrepreneurial university" (as Henry Etzkowitz, a professor of sociology with the State University of New York, names it), which "approaches the Baconian ideal of 'Solomon's House,' a multipurpose theoretical and practical research development agency for its society."[10] Whether this signals a new era of "democratic corporatism" or something worse, it may be well to remember another fabled visit, this time of Gulliver to the Academy of Lagado. Jonathan Swift was mocking the Royal Society for its sometimes silly schemes a century after *The New Atlantis.* In Lagado, there are projects "for extracting Sunbeams out of Cucumbers" and reducing "human Excrement to its original Food." Why, there's even an Automata Data of sorts, in the form of a "Project for improving speculative Knowledge by practical and mechanical Operations." The machine, composed of "several Bits of Wood . . . linked together by slender Wires," was intended, when its forty Iron Handles were cranked, to generate enough random sentences "to give the World a compleat Body of all Arts and Sciences."[11]

After New Atlantis and Lagado, you may wonder if the future of knowledge I am considering for the social sciences will lead to a world you would really want to live in. But it is well to remember that I do not intend for Automata Data to attain the proportions of a "compleat Body of all Arts and Sciences." It is only a way to mobilize those who are interested in doing something more to improve the public return on its investment in this knowledge economy of social science research.

In what follows I have unrealistically treated Automata Data as the Microsoft of public information providers. I do so for simplicity's sake, although it may well attract competitors in the knowledge field. It is, after all, the product of the postindustrial philosophy of this age, neatly summed up by the Chair and CEO of Intel Corporation, Andrew Grove, as "What technologically can be done has to be done, because it will be done."[12] Automata Data is my way of asking: if it is going to be done, is there more that we can do with it in the public interest? Can those who imagine themselves producing information in the public interest grab hold of these powerful information technologies to fulfill a greater part of this mission?

When it comes to the power of these new technologies, a good case in point is *data mining*. Data mining entails the automated processing of large electronic databases made up of the information collected on individuals by corporations, governments, and other institutions. Although I deal with it in more detail in the chapter on technologies of knowledge, let me return to the earlier example of breast cancer research to consider how a technology such as data mining might serve Automata Data. A recent Norwegian study on the relationship between exercise and breast cancer, which made the front page of the papers, tracked 25,000 women over a fourteen-year-period not only for their level of physical activity, but for their diets, weights, menarche, number of children, and age at which these women had their first child, as well as the incidence of breast cancer.[13] It was found that women who engaged in four or more hours of exercise a week reduced their risk of breast cancer by 37 percent.

This seems straightforward and reassuring, although the reporter points out that a dozen smaller studies on the influence of exercise have been conducted, "none of which taken alone, was conclusive," while this study, too, "was not definitive." What needs to be made clear, however, is that while this is all true, research that correlates habits and health is about managing risk and probabilities, rather than establishing the definitive, irrevocable logic of cause and effect. Given the continuing mysteries around the disease processes of cancer, pursuing ways of reducing the risks associated with the condition are to be welcomed. And Automata Data would not change any of that.

What it would do, as I envision it, is create a permanent and dynamic site for reviewing the social science and epidemiological research on cancer, and it would do so in such a way that rather than feeling exasperated by the less than definitive knowledge available, the public would at least be able to feel confident that they are in on what is known. Automata Data would not only provide the consolation, however slight that may prove, of knowing what is currently known, but would also invite participation in the public push to know more in one area rather than another.

Yet another potential contribution Automata Data could make, using the example of the Norwegian study, is to ensure that new technologies of data gathering and analysis being used for commercial purposes might be directed to the benefit of research. The information gathered, at great expense, from participants in this research study is also being collected electronically for women across the industrialized world by a range of agencies. For example, credit-card data records household diets, athletic clothing purchases, and fitness club memberships, while medical records have childbirth dates, family medical histories, and general health status. Exposure to urban pollution and to occupational hazards can be tracked through housing and employment records. With the participants' consent, and encryption of the data to protect individual identities, data mining software could be set up to analyze patterns and draw researchers' attention to anomalies. The data would be incomplete in places and would represent a very rough approximation of, for example, women's diet within a household's consumption. It may require follow-up inquiries. But with large samples, messy data is a far less significant issue. The resulting analysis could provide powerful indicators of what makes a difference on an international scale, and in a few years time it might even provide an indication of whether public knowledge about the research itself made a difference to women.

This automated data gathering would in all likelihood not lead to a cure for breast cancer, of course. It might, however, provide the public with a far more helpful and comprehensive picture of what has been studied and what has been found. It might extend the range of factors considered while giving more people the chance to join in this effort to learn more about reducing the risk of this disease. Current efforts have reduced breast cancer deaths by 10 percent over the last five years (although the rate is disturbingly unchanged for African American women).[14] There are also encouraging new preventive drug treatments, using tamoxifen and raloxifene, becoming available to women.[15] Still, devising ways of increasing the order and system among the vast array of research programs already underway in health, no less than in the other areas in which the social sciences are gathering data, could only help more people take advantage of what is known, as well as address potential inequities in health care.

When it comes to fighting crime or selling potato chips, there is no lack of concern with improving the coordination of data sources.[16] Insurance companies are purchasing police information about property theft and damage and using it to calculate their rates. This goes on despite public objections to trafficking in personal and identifiable electronic information, which in 1991 forced the Lotus Corporation to cancel sale of its MarketPlace CD-ROM which contained credit-rating information on 120 million people. Such electronic information on people continues to be gathered and sold, although it no longer draws as much attention. New Internet privacy standards are beginning to emerge over such issues as the information you leave behind after visiting a web site.

The critical difference with the automated data gathering I envision Automata Data performing is that people would have the option of donating their encrypted data knowing that it was in the public interest to conduct such research. They would be able to judge the results of this participation as well as participate in setting the research agenda. This condition of access to public and private databases for research purposes would certainly be subject to government regulation. At this point, for example, there are forty bills before the U.S. Congress aimed at improving a citizen's right to privacy, and Automata Data would only have a greater chance of success if people knew that their privacy was properly protected while they were contributing to the greater good.[17] That and the civil liberties unions would ensure that Automata Data retain its license to use this voluntarily contributed and encrypted data for research only if its processes remained open to public scrutiny. Its work might well have to be overseen by the likes of a Data Protection Agency to ensure the fair use of data and equal access to information, principally through the corporation's *pro bono* information generation and other forms of community service work.

One measure of the public's potential response to such a request for volunteering data comes from a recent Canadian poll that found 81 percent of those asked were in favor of allowing researchers access to their anonymous medical records.[18] If many are willing organ donors, surely more would agree to be data donors. What easier way could there be to contribute to the common good than to allow the anonymous use of one's credit card swipes, one's health and education records? What better way to ensure that the technology is not simply used merely for more marketing?[19]

However, the clever use of technology will not put an end to the shortcomings of social science research. Whatever hope we hold out for the benefits and consolation of knowledge lies not with the machines but in our own hands and heads, in what we come to expect of this knowledge and the ends to which we turn it. Certainly, Dr. Frankenstein and others would warn us all against these tendencies toward trumpeting technology's yet-to-be-realized powers. The machines are not the answer to our dreams; nor need they be the source of our nightmares. The machines drive us only as we are already driven, and we do not seem headed to anywhere we have not already been. After all, these new realms of cyberspace and info-byways are directed more often than not at satisfying such deep-seated desires as finding the used car of one's dreams on the 'net, or emailing contract negotiations back and forth while riding in taxicabs to airports. To consider the speculative and perhaps monstrous prospects of an Automata Data Corporation is to wonder at the public value of the social sciences' tireless research enterprise. It is to return to what drives this disciplinary inquiry, to make sure that this is where we want it headed, even as we better understand that this is all we can hope for along the way.

3

Information Explosion

Automata data is based on a very simple information principle. More information does not necessarily lead to greater wisdom. Or in this case, the substantial accumulation of research in the social sciences does not appear to be making people correspondingly wiser. After all, where is the evidence that the accretion of facts, figures, analyses, and interpretations is leading to a similar upswell of benefit or consolation for those on whose behalf the research is undertaken? This headlong production of research is simply *not* being matched by an equal application of talent and energy to rendering the resulting knowledge intelligible and accessible to a broader public.

The result is that research just goes on and on, with little overall understanding of the whole and the part, the direction and the context. And this is not just true of an uninformed public; many of us within the social sciences would be hard pressed to describe with any confidence the line of progress in our field.[1] The public might fairly ask why it is so hard, if every aspect of their social lives is subject to some form of inquiry, to get a straight answer from the social sciences when it is needed. Come a critical juncture in social policy, like a renewed determination to curb smoking among the young, and all the light that the social sciences can cast on the leading strategy of raising the price of cigarettes is a few contradictory studies or "unproven data," as the headline of the day had it.[2] The public sigh is almost audible. Don't researchers have to reconcile discrepancies? Don't they have to determine whether the disagreement is in principle, interpretation, or method? Isn't there some responsibility for following up on this work?

The sense of exasperation is all the more apparent and demoralizing when one considers just how much research the social sciences conduct. By way of very crude measures, I would calculate that of the 600,000 university faculty now teaching in the United States, a little more than a quarter are working in social science disciplines or related fields, such as education, law, and business. In annual surveys, 80 percent of all faculty report that they regularly engage in research, with fully a quarter of these claiming they put in more than nine hours a week on it. All of this translates for the social sciences into somewhat more than 100,000 articles and 30,000 book chapters or books a year.[3] In addition to faculty research, graduate students in my field of education alone produce more than 6,000 dissertations a year directed at understanding and improving the quality of teaching and learning.[4]

What all of this means in terms of accumulated research can be gauged by considering the holdings of that great knowledge warehouse, the Harvard University library system. The entire collection runs to 13 million volumes, to which the library system adds a breathtaking 275,000 volumes each year. This is not simply the wholesale accumulation of everything that has been published; rather, it reflects the selections of a library staff of more than 900 people, working with an annual budget of $68 million, dedicated to building the best scholarly collection in the world. Harvard's subscription to more than 90,000 serials offers another annual measure of global research activities. It is well to remember that only a century ago, Princeton's library was open but an hour a week—but then, the entire nation produced only a single dissertation in the year 1871.[5]

While faculty and graduate students have increased in number over the years, they have done so at nowhere near the rate of increase in the number of journals. Between 1970 and 1990, the number of serials listed in Ulrich's exhaustive catalog increased by 50 percent.[6] In biology, psychology, and English, journal space nearly doubled between 1972 and 1988, although faculty numbers in these disciplines increased only slightly during that time.[7] To take one of the more prolific scholarly arenas, historians now have some 5,000 journals to carry and inform their work. How can a historian keep up, if not by further specializing, reading and writing more about less?[8] How can one tell the journals apart, I wonder as I notice invitations on my desk to subscribe to the *Journal of Research on Computing in Education* and the *Journal of Educational Computing Research*?

The reasons for the current growth in research range from required program evaluations in areas of social policy to the reward structure of the academic professions. The result is not so much a free marketplace of ideas as an endless and overloaded flea market, full of wondrous goods but with few apparent organizing principles governing what turns up. Better to be surprised and delighted by what you come across than to come looking for something you need. Or to go at it another way, it can be like the joke about the restaurant that may serve awful food but at least there's plenty of it.

The question at hand is whether the career-determining rite of publication, which is the most immediate and demonstrable benefit of this proliferation of journals, is matched by much less quantifiablecontributions to knowledge. Among the hyperinflationary signs that the age of the journal may be peaking, if not passing, is the system developed by physicists for circulating what they know among their colleagues. This system and its users appear poised, in fact, to put the traditional journal system out of business through a strange concoction of automated archiving and distribution by which they circulate their research. Many physicist now send electronic versions of their articles—known as *E-prints*—to a database set up for automated storage, cataloguing, and retrieval. Now not only can you instantly access from your desktop a paper such as "Inflationary Reheating in Grand Unified Theories"—you can even observe animated three-dimensional graphings of its data.[9] This system began as a "preprint" service for articles awaiting publication, but physicists now send their pieces directly, without going through traditional journal publication. According to IBM physicist Charles Bennett, "there has been no serious problem of people submitting inappropriate matter, or papers so badly written as to chiefly constitute a waste of the reader's time," to which he adds, "I can't say that of the mail I get in my mailbox or my E-mail inbox."[10] The extended physics Website-database is visited by 35,000 users worldwide daily.[11]

Automated archive services are now being set up in economics and linguistics as well as in other sciences. According to physicist Paul Ginsparg, who initiated E-prints, this dynamic service has reduced the critical role of the blind referee to the flow of knowledge. Every reader is now a peer reviewer, and papers that are successfully challenged are replaced with a note explaining that the work was withdrawn by the authors; some papers are simply ignored. Knowledge is measured not by the wave of the referee's hand, but by the use of the work by others, while the archive becomes the total library. In his enthusiasm, Ginsparg does point to an opening for an Automata Data of physics, noting "a pressing need for [the] organization of intellectual value . . . [which] leaves significant opportunities for any agency willing to listen to what researchers want and need."[12] On the other hand, Jerome Kasirer, current editor of the *New England Journal of Medicine*, cautions that "physics is a small community of people, and what they put on their Web site is not going to affect the health of thousands or millions of people."[13] For his part, Ginsparg insists that the issue is whether publishers or professors control access. Another physicist, Nobel laureate Murray Gell-Mann, asks, "How can we improve our reward system for excellence in filtering, interpreting, and synthesizing the vast body of so-called information with which we are deluged?"[14] Add to that the wants and needs of a public for whom social scientists believe they are producing something of intellectual value and you have the case for launching this corporation for public knowledge that I am calling Automata Data.

One even finds university administrators, who are often first among those who seem to demand publication for its own sake, beginning to recognize that, as an end in itself, more research may not be all that much more productive. Ralph Norman, Vice Chancellor at the University of Tennessee, for example, goes on at length about how we cannot help but find that the "*intellectual sensorium* is clogged, glutted, surfeited, full, overstuffed, bloated, teeming, overabundant, overflowing."[15] Too much knowledge in an Age of Information? Do we name our ages by our excesses? Is there anyone, outside of gangster movies, who is accused of knowing too much? Surely the surfeit is not the whole of the problem. Having stepped out of his academic specialization to take charge of a university as a whole, Vice Chancellor Norman speaks of an economy of attention that is bound to be frustrated not only by the scale of this enterprise, but by the difficulty of determining—and he is using the humanities as his reference point—the cumulative effect of this much scholarship.

Addressing the limits of attention and information in the social sciences, John Horgan, in his portentous *The End of Science*, presses Clifford Geertz into confessing the true nature of much research as clever busy work, or as he quotes Geertz: "There is not much assurance or sense of closure, not even much of a sense of knowing what one precisely *is* after, in so indefinite a quest, amid such various people, over such a diversity of times. But it is an excellent way, interesting, dismaying, useful, amusing, to spend a life."[16] My take is that we should be doing something that introduces a sense of the necessary into Geertz's list. Otherwise, this "indefinite quest" is about pumping out just so much "data smog," to borrow the title of David Shenk's book.[17] Among the many examples of "information glut" Shenk points to the more than 100,000 studies estimated to have been conducted on depression. When information reaches that scale it becomes easy to imagine it following its own law of diminishing returns.

Think of it this way. When there is only one study on depression, to speak hypothetically, it is bound to have its limitations, certainly, but limitations that can easily be comprehended and taken into consideration. When there are three studies, it is relatively easy to compare alternative explanations and to see how each study stands in relation to the others. When there are ten studies, the value of the individual studies is diminished, and the coherence of the whole body of research suffers, to the degree that the more recent studies fail to incorporate or address that whole. When there are 1,000 studies, the value of each study begins to approach the minuscule, especially as each one strains to relate to the rest of the field. What then of 100,000 studies?[18] The law of diminishing returns does not simply drive the value of a single study toward zero; studies begin to assume a negative value as they add to the frustration felt by those who feel that they should be better served by all of this research activity. The answer is not to limit the number of studies, obviously. The hope that I see is in finding a means of introducing greater coordination within every phase of the research activity. The goal would be to ensure that each study is able to find its place within the greater comprehensibility of the whole, not only as it complements existing work, but as it goes on to challenge research traditions or to strike off in new directions. But it would be better to offer an example of what an Automata Data could contribute to the research surrounding a particular significant educational issue.

When it comes to how this proliferation works in practice, there is no group that social science research has serve as poorly in America as children who come to school speaking a mother tongue other than English. The research on bilingual education offers a most disheartening failure of so much research for so little cumulative knowledge. Despite the wealth of research on bilingual education over the last couple of decades, it is impossible to sort out with any confidence the consequences and opportunities posed by the range of bilingual programs in place across America. In 1990, this issue affected 14 percent of American children—some 6,300,000 of them—and that number has only been increasing.[19] While President Clinton and the Congress, under the Bilingual Education Act of 1968, increased federal financing for these programs to $354 million in 1997, the people of California have voted to replace bilingual programs with one-year English immersion. The California referendum was initiated by Ron Unz, who was able to point, in the statute on which the public voted, "to costly experimental language programs whose failure over the past two decades is demonstrated by the current high drop-out rate and low English literacy levels of many immigrant children."[20] The Hispanic community was clearly divided on the issue, with some parents boycotting bilingual programs and others raising accusations of "ethnic cleansing" when their school boards voted against any further funding for bilingual programs.[21]

This is just the sort of critical issue one might expect the social sciences to help people sort out. What are the strengths and weaknesses of different bilingual and English immersion programs? Are dropout rates and test scores directly attributable to bilingual versus monolingual programs? What are the interactions of the two languages and the different ways of handling the balance between them? How do we resolve the tensions between mother tongue and national language? Help us to understand the basis of differing findings and results in the research, the public might ask. Show us the figures, some might say, tell us what comes of these programs, and we'll decide how the children should be educated. Instead what they get is "notoriously inconclusive" research, as the *New York Times* calls it, which enables the

Unz initiative in California and other attacks on bilingual education to make selective claims to reason and research—claims I want to play out in some detail here.[22]

In a *New York Times'* op-ed piece, Diane Ravitch, senior fellow at the Brookings Institute, takes what has become the standard position. She brushes off bilingual education as a "dismal failure."[23] She argues against continuing any form of bilingual education and in favor of placing those students who come to school speaking another language in English immersion classes. She backs her stance by citing research conducted by the New York Board of Education in which 90 percent of students who started bilingual education in grade six "were unable to pass an English language test after three years of bilingual instruction." She also points to studies of higher dropout rates among Hispanics, especially those who do not adequately speak English. English is the sole measure of educational success here, with little thought given to utilizing the students' existing linguistic strengths on the road to proficiency in another language.

Ravitch asks that the parents of these students be told about "the poor track record of bilingual education" so that they can pull their children out of such programs. As it now stands, "parents must navigate an elaborate bureaucratic process to withdraw children from bilingual education." While I clearly support going public with the relevant research and reducing the bureaucratic hurdles that prevent parents from exercising their authority, something larger is amiss here. The problem is that the research on bilingual education is nowhere near as definitive as Ravitch suggests, whether in its condemnation of existing programs or in its identification of what works. The social sciences analysis of bilingual education exemplifies just how bad it can get with too much research adding up to too little public value.

Let me start with the good news. Of all the areas of inquiry in the social sciences, the study of education has the advantage of a federally funded and electronically accessible clearinghouse of research. ERIC (Educational Resources Information Center) contains more than 850,000 abstracts of documents and journal articles. It is the world's largest source of educational information. Established in 1966, and supported by the U.S. Department of Education, Office of Educational Research and Improvement, and the National Library of Education, ERIC now operates a World Wide Website that offers researchers the ability to search the last ten years of records free of charge. It is currently putting the full text of articles online, to be available on a pay-per-download basis. ERIC represents its own version of an Automata Data, with lessons to be learned about what the organization of research requires.[24]

After reading Ravitch's piece, I searched the ERIC database with a request for studies on the *evaluation* of *bilingual education*. This quickly produced a list of 650 abstracts.[25] The abstracts are not in a standard format, which often makes it difficult to assess who and what has been studied, and one is always on the verge of being overwhelmed in trying to sort out how the studies relate and what they add up to. ERIC has recognized this problem of too much information with its too-long lists, and has commissioned research digests on topics such as bilingual education. On turning to these digests, I found that they made their own observations on the disarray that besets research in this field. These digests are able to cull out the characteristics of successful programs, such as "supportive whole-school contexts" and "high expectations," but these recommendations are so general in nature as to be of limited value to teachers and parents trying to make critical decisions about which way to turn.[26]

The federal government has not missed the point on this want of organization and has established agencies specifically to deal with bilingual education, such as the National Clearinghouse for Bilingual Education, funded by the U.S. Department of Education's Office of Bilingual Education and Minority Languages Affairs with a mandate "to collect, analyze, and disseminate information relating to the effective education of linguistically and culturally diverse learners in the U.S."[27] Still, the overabundance of uncoordinated research activity makes it hardly surprising that Ravitch could dismiss bilingual education as a failure without much fear of contradiction. Certainly, the research is not doing well.

The major reviews of bilingual education research reveal that a great many of the studies routinely conducted on these programs—evaluations have been a legally required component of federally funded programs since 1977—do not qualify as sound studies, while those that stand are in much disagreement about the value of the various bilingual programs in use.[28] Guidelines and systems for creating easily manageable evaluation models have been proposed, while nothing appears to have really caught on as the standard on a national scale.[29] Centrifugal forces rule— and so it has been since the early years of bilingual education.

In the 1970s, Frederick Shaw, a director of research with the New York City Board of Education, found that for every study that supported starting with the students' mother tongue, there was another recommending that the child start school in the national language.[30] It is much the same two decades later. In 1992, Gary Cziko, a psychologist at the University of Illinois, published a review of six large-scale studies that attempted to evaluate how well bilingual education programs worked. He found a similarly mixed bag of results.[31] While students in some of the transitional bilingual programs (with students passing through on their way to regular English programs) did do better than those who did not have the advantage of these programs, there were other similar programs that had no effect, and some that proved detrimental to the students' progress.

The problem is that these studies tend to cancel each other out or disappear in the grip of a meta-analysis that attempts to cull their different measures into a single set of calculations. Had there been a far more coordinated approach to the design, conduct, and analysis of the research in the first place, the differences in their findings could be analyzed more confidently, and could serve as a far more helpful guide to those attempting to sort through the impact of these programs.

Given the current confusion over what works (in what ways, where, and for whom), we need to stop and ask whether some common ground can be found between what it takes to root local initiatives within specific communities and the need for developing a more global understanding. The underlying questions are the same. What do we know about running different sorts of second-language programs in various communities? How do we make sense of the differences in the programs, in their goals and methods, and the differences in the evaluation studies? My assumption is that different types of programs can be evaluated on their own terms, as long as efforts are made to find a point of comparison with other programs. This would be the task of an Automata Data. It would work with researchers and their sponsors to ensure that the research not only made a statement about a particular program but contributed to the larger and common good.

As it now stands, we can at least establish that the current state of the research allows for sweeping critiques of bilingual education like the one offered by Diane Ravitch. Individual studies may serve specific programs, and insights are gained about the experiences of students and teachers. But from where I stand, what is decidedly "dismal," to use Ravitch's word for the programs' record, is our failure to learn more about how to garner the value of a greater part of this research activity. What is dismal is that this much research produces so little help in making sense of bilingual education. Surely more could be done to provide a more complete and coherent picture of how various programs work—and fail to work.

The simplistic solution to this dilemma is to propose that an organization like Automata Data extract whatever coherence it can from the existing body of research, sorting out the findings and claims in relation to one another, as the starting point for developing a far more systematic and coordinated approach to demonstrating what takes place in different sorts of programs and circumstances. Among so many studies, the breakdown in coherence, resulting in the notorious inconclusiveness, is a cumulative effect. Establishing a means to greater coherence needs to become the major research focus before another year is spent pursuing hundreds of research studies on bilingual education at a cost of millions of dollars.[32] The aim here is not the definitive study, identifying the best program, or even a reassuring set of best practices. It is to prevent this body of research from canceling itself out in a bundle of confusions and contradictions.

This is to assume that even studies that arrive at diametrically opposed results in examining similar phenomena may do so for good reason (rather than because of mistakes in method), and that the very basis of these different results can be rendered intelligible, as a difference in goals and values, which can also help people understand the issues. So it is that one bilingual program may succeed slightly better with students in the sciences, while another offers advantages in the social language skills, and a third proves somewhat stronger in preserving the home language. For despite the focus on achievement scores, research needs to remain sensitive to the sense of cultural belonging schools can foster, of the sort reflected by Martha Leon, a housekeeper whose daughter is in a fourth-grade bilingual program in Santa Ana, California. Leon reports that "My daughter is learning English, but because of the Spanish, I feel the school is mine."[33] English immersion programs may speed up social integration within the school's Anglophone culture, while two-way bilingualism enables a sharing of the linguistic wealth of the community among all the children. The differences among programs are based on differences in values, while differences in results are a matter of probabilities, and often of only the slightest advantage, but that need not deter a growing understanding of what can be learned about these programs.

Parents, teachers, and others can use this tentative, unfolding knowledge to work together on what they want for their communities, knowing that the research will not decide but only inform the process. Informed dexision making becomes a right afforded by the social sciences through Automata Data. We can make it a law across the land that a $1.79 jar of mayonnaise has to be labeled with "Nutrition Facts," down to its potential contribution to my daily sodium allowance. A federal agency decided that it was critical for us to be informed of the pertinent mayonnaise facts, with an eye to managing such risks as heart disease. Given this educational approach to public knowledge about diet, it seems only reasonable to ask, before entering my child into the educational environment that will occupy the better part of the next three years of her life, that I receive a similar level of information on the potential impact of an educational program, whether that research is based on test scores, teacher interviews, or multimedia narratives of the classroom experience.

With such information at hand, the public can begin the real exercise of understanding, of discussing and deciding how best to balance educational values and create programs that serve community interests. Diane Ravitch will still hold that English comes first in educating this nation and that bilingual education interferes with that, and I will still ask why parents cannot have their children retain more of the language that has held their family for generations. But we could at least turn to Automata Data to test our empirical claims about the programs. We could consult it on a regular basis to see if results are changing or new patterns are emerging. We could challenge it to investigate unanswered questions and explain seemingly contradictory studies.

My concern is not just to marshal somehow the great accumulation after the fact, for this push to improve the intelligibility of the research enterprise will only work if it begins with how the research is conceived, designed, and planned. Controlled explosions are the secret of successfully harnessing nuclear energy, and they require constant monitoring, with lots of technological support, so that what is initially unleashed is usefully contained from the very outset. But I also know that the containment I am proposing for the social sciences is, first of all, a matter of this research community recognizing the need to improve the public value of the knowledge we work so hard to construct. One critical human response to this explosion and proliferation could be characterized as disciplinary fragmentation, which would contain the overload by fostering social science subdisciplines and schools of thought that afford, amid the confusion, an insider's sense of community and shelter. What it does for those who reside outside the discipline is add to what needs to be overcome and sorted out if we are to make any sense of the knowledge offered.

The Fragmentation

Princeton anthropologist Clifford Geertz, although better known for his analysis of Balinese cockfights, has more recently cast his well-trained eye on his field's sister discipline of psychology. The result is a quick-sketch ethnography of advanced intellectual fragmentation: "From the outside, at least, it does not look like a single field, divided into schools and specialties in the usual way. It looks like an assortment of disparate and disconnected inquiries classed together because they all make reference in some way or another to something or other called 'mental functioning.' Dozens of characters in search of a play."[34] Whether any field of knowledge today can be said to be divided in the "usual way," and what the usual divisions of knowledge really are, is a little hard to imagine. For example, is Geertz's own discipline, which he calls "eclectic" in the article, any more coherent?[35]

Geertz goes on to note that the American Psychological Association has forty-nine divisions. He is especially dismayed by the instability of the field's theoretical range: "The wide swing between behaviorist, psychometric, cognitivist, depth psychological, topological developmentalist, neurological developmentalist, neurological, evolutionist, and culturalist conceptions of the subject have made being a psychologist an unsettled occupation, subject not only to fashion, as are all the human sciences, but also to sudden and frequent reversals of course."[36] What he doesn't note is how Auguste Comte, considerably more than a century earlier, voiced similar complaints as he strove to get sociology under way, objecting to the fruitless "multitude of schools" who were given to "metaphors mistaken for reasoning."[37]

Geertz's theme here is the discipline's lack of discipline, and what that might cost in coherence, all of which is compounded by the energetic quality of a profession on the make: "It takes either a preternaturally focused, dogmatical person, who can shut out any ideas but his own, or a mercurial, hopelessly inquisitive one, who can keep dozens of them in play at once, to remain upright amid this tumble of programs, promises, proclamations."[38] His report from the field, as it were, conveys wonderfully well the divergence and contest among ideas, of free intellectual enterprise within a competitive marketplace. Psychology appears to be searching for a coherent picture of mental functioning, and yet everything about the field is structured against such coherence and set to reward the competition.

Geertz's mini-anthropology of psychology took place within the context of reviewing Jerome Bruner's book *The Culture of Education*.[39] Bruner has moved, in his own conceptual development as a psychologist, out of cognitivism and into the semi-anthropological form of cultural psychology. His new tack is of special interest here for how it would portray the child as, in Bruner's words, "an epistemologist as well as a learner," with the result that she "gradually comes to appreciate that she is acting not directly *on* 'the world' but on beliefs she holds *about* that world."[40] The startling aspect of this claim, one Geertz skates readily over, is that according to Bruner children might be said to *appreciate* that they cannot know reality directly but can only

hold beliefs about it, which makes them truly discerning episte-
mologists. That it appears to have taken the senior Bruner a lifetime to arrive at this appreciation does not seem to enter into his
analysis. It should at least warn us of how tempting it is to make
of children what we have finally become.

What we are left with is Bruner's image of children making
epistemological sense of their own lives, against Geertz's sense of
psychology's fragmentation. It might seem to make child's play
of this academic worry about knowledge. Yet it speaks as well to
the sense of the loss represented by this fragmentation that is
everywhere present in our efforts to act on our beliefs about the
world, to return to Bruner, through research and other forms of
intellectual activity: "The communication and coordination of
these scattered fragments of knowledge," Thomas Sowell writes,
"is one of the basic problems—perhaps *the* basic problem—of
any society, as well as of its constituent institutions and relationships."[41] The social sciences have been struggling with this problem for some time, as D. L. Eckberg and L. Hill Jr. noted some
twenty years ago:

> What we often find is research modeled upon no other research at
> all, upon a short, soon-extinguished line of research or upon a single
> theorist's speculation. . . . We find constant bickering and debate,
> but little agreement. The lack of agreement affects operationaliza-
> tion and manipulation of concepts, such that different research re-
> quires different, often incommensurable data. The concepts seem to
> change from study to study.[42]

Against the fragmentations among research studies on a given
topic, as well as against the fragmentation that divides and subdi-
vides disciplines (themselves divisions of the larger knowledge
enterprise), I am suggesting that we consider establishing struc-

tures that act as countervailing forces. These structures should be directed not at seeking the unity of all knowledge but at mapping the diversity, the ways of knowing, so that one can find a bridge from Bruner's cognitive psychology to his cultural psychology, and in so doing trace the educational consequences of emphasizing culture over cognition. Foreseeing which sorts of bridges and maps within the divisions of knowledge would contribute most to the public intelligibility of what the social sciences have to offer would be the work of an Automata Data. It would be driven by constant experiment and inquiry aimed at striking that balance between the forces of fragmentation and the epistemological drive for the greater sense of things, which first shows itself, as Bruner points out, in the young child.

Although each discipline has its own traditions when it comes to living with the fragmentation of knowledge, there are times when what goes on in one area can ring remarkably true for the others. Or so it would seem on reading what the outspoken molecular geneticist Richard Lewontin has to say about scientific hubris. His comments are from the intellectual battlefield of the *New York Review of Books* letters section. They are addressed to colleagues who took exception to his less than generous treatment of the Human Genome Project, which represents one of the major knowledge projects under way as we close out the millennium. Although Lewontin is addressing research on a molecular level, the social sciences suffer no less a temptation to go after the easier and less critical questions, while paying homage to "public faith and concrete investment," as he puts it:

No one can deny that whatever information can be obtained about one bit of the physical world has ramifications for the knowledge and manipulation of other parts. Often these ramifications are un-expected. Even more often, especially in those particularly compli-cated parts of the physical world constituted by living organisms, the knowledge that is accessible is separated from what we really want to understand by very hard questions whose answers we do not know how to obtain. At one time or another in their lives most scientists realize the extent of the separation but they also perceive, probably correctly, that public faith and concrete investment in science de-pend on a connection between knowledge and result that is much simpler. So they are led to make extravagant claims for the opera-tion of science, both for the objectivity and compelling power of a formulaic "scientific method" and for the direct applicability of elementary knowledge to problems of human welfare. When chal-lenged, they throw up an obfuscating cloud of quite interesting and sometimes even quite useful results of scientific investigation, in the hope that no one will notice the original problem has not been solved, or that it has, but by a pathway quite unrelated to what they have been doing.[43]

Lewontin poses not so much a critique as a *realpolitik* of research processes and funding that should give us pause in the social sci-ences. We too face the "very hard questions whose answers we do not know how to obtain." We are all devoted, whether in hard, soft, or human sciences, to producing "quite interesting and sometimes even quite useful results" that may not solve the origi-nal and more distressing problems, which will always require, well, more research.

I am hoping that the social sciences can mount a more con-certed effort at identifying with or against the public "what we really want to understand," before the research community is called, once too often, on those obfuscating research clouds. The necessary changes could be assisted through the corporate form of an Automata Data, which like New York University would claim to be "a private institution in the public service." But not necessarily. The real change needs to take place in the ethos and ethics under which we conduct research. E-prints and ERIC are responses to this need to improve how we manage what happens to what we know. However, I have not finished setting out either the public or the professional response to this information explosion, and how I hope to see through a device such as Automata Data the full range of research inquiry made available as a public resource, without sacrificing the social sciences' own democratic play of ideas about knowledge and its purposes.

4

....

Reading Exasperation

OVER BREAKFAST one morning while I was working on this book, I came across the front-page headline, "Phonics Reading Method Best, Study Finds: Whole-Language Approach Significantly Less Effective, Houston Research Shows."[1] I put my cereal spoon down. This really was news to me. After all, I had been involved in the great reading debate for nearly two decades, and on the side of the apparently "significantly less effective" whole-language approach, as the headline put it. In that time, educational research on learning to read tended to be divided between studies that supported children beginning the path to literacy with the phonetical letter-sound correspondences and those that supported starting with the rich story experiences of whole language. Although many teachers use aspects of both approaches in their teaching, these two nonetheless antithetical theories have divided educators for decades, with no shortage of research support, albeit of very different sorts, to be found on both sides. There had yet to emerge a definitive, irrefutable body of research that both sides would accept on what works best. It was a standoff, with loyalties running deep.

So I was a little surprised to find my newspaper that morning pronouncing the war over. We had lost and phonics had triumphed. It was now clear that the best way to become a reader is to first learn letter-sound correspondences. Whatever my alarm, I'm sure many a parent and teacher paused over the article, too, with most breathing a sigh of relief. Here was an issue that had long been a source of exasperation for parents and public. As it stands, measures of literacy levels among the young have not been terribly encouraging, and this contest between reading methods has not appeared helpful. Finally, parents and public must have thought, these things do get settled. Now teachers can move on, knowing the best way to teach our children.

While I am obviously more than sympathetic toward this public desire for a straight answer on such questions, the sudden and decisive victory reported that morning seemed a little unlikely. By the same token, I imagine you may be a little suspicious of my motives for trying to snatch victory from the hands of my phonic-backing colleagues, if only to prolong the great reading debate. But with such caution in mind, I ask that you follow this sometimes frustrating tale of knowledge in the social sciences, to see what more (and less) can be expected of those sciences through a vehicle such as an Automata Data Corporation, on such critical matters as learning how to read.

The newspaper article reported on a presentation by Barbara Foorman, an educational psychologist at the University of Houston, to the American Association for the Advancement of Science. Foorman's study of reading teaching involved 375 "low-achieving, poor Grade One students," divided into two groups for reading class, with a "phonics group" focused on the skills needed to sound out new words, and a "whole language group" focused on using words in the context of stories they were trying to read and write. Foorman found that, on U.S. national norm tests, 43 percent of the phonics students scored at or above the average for their grade, compared to 30 percent of the whole-language students. Even more dramatically, 33 percent of the whole-language students scored at the very low end of the reading ability scale, with scores indicating the possibility of "learning disabilities" (set at 2.5 words or fewer on a 50-word list), compared to only 6 percent of the phonics students at the same level. Foorman is quoted as noting that "these percentiles are quite startling and you don't usually find these effects in social science research very often."

What you don't usually find in social science research—by way of unequivocal results—is exactly what the public is looking for. Foorman achieves these striking effects by, first of all, carefully comparing the two programs with common measures, although her focus on word lists so clearly favors the phonic methods with their word attack skills that the results are bound to be predictably significant. By way of contrast, the research I conducted some years ago on grade one students in both programs demonstrated just how much more sentence-level writing students might be expected to do in the whole-language classrooms than in phonics classrooms, which was associated with a stronger grammatical sense among the whole-language students.[2] The comparative quality and public value of both Foorman's and my studies would have been helped by assessing the students' learning using measures directly related to the claims of both phonics and whole-language programs.

The point is that a phenomenon as complex as literacy can be variously taught, researched, understood, measured, and compared. Rather than seeking to establish the one best method, the social sciences would do better to assemble insights into this complexity so that people can inform and perhaps expand their vision of literacy and how the schools can best promote it.

An interesting feature of this report on the Foorman study is that it includes the response of the participating children's parents. They were informed of the research results (itself an all too rare move), and were then given a choice of which program to place their children in: "The literate parents who read the note when it came home put their children in the phonics program," Professor Foorman told the reporter, in as fine an example as one might find on how quickly scientists can leave their scientific methods behind when it comes to getting behind an idea they believe in. (If the parents were literate and read the note, she seems to have assumed, they put their children in the phonics class, and those who didn't, therefore, were illiterate non-note-readers or worse.)

Other indications that the results of the study were being taken very seriously outside the academy came from George W. Bush, governor of Texas. The article reports he asked Professor Foorman and her colleagues to address the heads of the state's Schools of Education so that new generations of teachers might benefit from these findings. Others at Foorman's American Association for the Advancement of Science presentation joined in the critique of whole language, with a psychologist from McGill University, Maggie Bruck, attacking its "anti-scientific platform."[3]

As if to exemplify my earlier calculus of research value—by which the multiplication of studies reduces the value of each study—the newspaper report on the Foorman study is all the more reassuring because it considers her study in isolation, ignoring several decades' worth of other studies on reading education. It leaves the impression that now we know what works in learning to read. Truth and public have been served on the basis of a single study.

Within two weeks of the newspaper's report on the Foorman study, the same newspaper carried a defense of whole language on its op-ed page.[4] In the civil language of the academy, the four professors of education who authored the piece declare their "serious difficulties with the Foorman study," taking exception to the word-list approach and to Foorman's position as a "longtime advocate of 'pure phonics.'" They counter her study by citing a two-year research project which they claim demonstrated how whole-language students can do at least as well as phonics students in phonics exercises and better on other reading measures.[5] The four defenders of whole language declare, finally, that "the issue is not whether to teach phonics but the timing of the instruction and the conditions under which these skills are taught." For them, given their defense of whole language, the debate between phonics and whole language is "neither interesting nor enlightening." And therefore it should go away?

Clearly, the debate is nothing but interesting and enlightening when it comes to the nature of knowledge in the social sciences. It represents a hope for understanding what divides perspectives on reading. While both sides want to move on, *as if* the issue had been resolved by one piece of research or another, their continuing disagreement belies the greater truth that we want many things of reading and its instruction. As long as reading instruction is treated by both sides as a contest of ideas that can only and ultimately have one winner, then we have to face a long road of contradictory claims and findings, with little ability to compare studies fairly. And the public is not particularly amused by this strategy.

New York Times' reporter Jacques Steinberg fears no contradiction when he claims, for example, that "precious little educational research is done by anyone who is not advocating a particular point of view—leaving little middle ground."[6] Steinberg has little trouble finding former school chancellors and Harvard Deans of Education to back up his complaint when it comes to research on reading methods. Yet he also cites the whole-language movement leader, Kenneth Goodman of the University of Arizona, who blames the public for the lack of a middle ground, pointing to its desire for "one right program."[7] This finger-pointing should be enough to send the public's exasperation needle bouncing up again.

The nature of this public interest in knowing what research has to offer was the topic of the *Globe and Mail* editorial, "Hooked on Phonics," that followed the report on the Foorman study.[8] The paper held the government responsible for informing people about such research results as the best method for teaching reading. For a generation, the editorial complains, the "weapon of choice [in the debate over reading] has been assertion rather than argument." It places a good deal of weight on the parents' response in the Foorman study—namely, that an unspecified number, when told of the study and given the choice, switched their children to the phonics program: "That tells us something important about how people react to reliable scientific information. Parents want their children to succeed. Prove to them that whole language is the best method, and they will gladly endorse the school board's decision to employ it." The editorial concludes by reasserting the value of getting such reassuring studies as Foorman's into the hands of the public: "Are provincial governments doing enough to put such information in the hands of students and parents? The answer, at this point, is no." There is much to be taken from this unequivocal *no*. The editorial expresses the level of frustration over the public's failure to receive reliable scientific information. It holds the governments responsible for providing this information, especially as it bears on such critical areas as education.[9]

Automata Data would, of course, do all in its power to address these concerns. It would seek to earn government support in making it easier for parents, practitioners, and public to gain access to the arguments and proofs that bear on such matters as how children learn to read. But I do not believe this has anything to do with finding the *best method*, as if there could be a unified or singular truth about reading that the social sciences are (always) about to uncover. We have learned many things about reading over the years. Neurophysiological processes have been identified. Word-attack strategies do work consistently. Children do feel pride authoring their own Mother's Day cards. They can imitate the pattern of their favorite books in their own earliest writing. Yet these discoveries, which represent consistent and replicable truths, still operate within different interpretations of what counts as reading. Because reading encompasses both the sounding out of a word and the interpreting of a culture, it is unlikely that there would be a single best method for learning to read.

Instead, an Automata Data would have to help people recognize just how reading researchers are engaged in studying what they believe is most important about reading. The division between phonics and whole language is about different ways of understanding reading. To say that reading begins with the accurate decoding of individual words is quite different from starting with an array of children's literature, shared in "big book" format. To begin teaching the letter-sound correspondences does not preclude introducing students to literature and other meaningful narratives with which whole-language teachers initiate the reading experiences of their students. Even as teachers inevitably mix and match methods, they are bound to place different weights on one aspect or another of what reading appears to be about. Each method can claim its point of principal effectiveness, and phonics with its concern for accuracy has tended to score more points with the general public.

As it happens, the students' ability in Foorman's study to read words off a 50-word list is exactly what instruction in phonics is designed to enable students to do.[10] What this says about the importance of reading is precisely what troubles the whole-language advocate, who is likely to hold up, by way of an illustration, a short story by Barry Udall which has in it a desperate character who finally finds himself sitting in his car "for over an hour reading the nutritional information on the back of his Coors."[11] Obviously his phonics training as a child was paying off, a far too sarcastic whole-language advocate might unfairly quip.

When I first got involved in the debate between reading camps I was so struck by its tempestuousness that I went looking for the historical origins of such a division. I became convinced that the rift between phonics and whole-language advocates represented a latter-day rejection of the rational and mechanistic sensibilities of the European Enlightenment by the organic and nature-bound interests of the Romantics. Out of rational and organic views of the world come visions not only of reading and learning, but of the child herself.[12] The child, with a phonics worksheet or a book in her hand, can be seen as the playground for the ideas driving the age. The social sciences can help us understand how such ideas work themselves out in history and philosophy, as well as in classrooms and children's lives. They can show that the method of teaching will not be decided by research, but should be the stuff of continuing public deliberation among communities, educators, and students, with children afforded the opportunities, as they currently are, for a wide range of learning experiences. This seems a more helpful intellectual project than pursuing a fight to the finish (that will never be finished) over the one best idea of reading.

Automata Data would offer the public greater understanding of the consequences of these different ideas about reading. It would arrange the research so that public and practitioners could see what comes of learning to read in this way or that, so that people could more confidently make decisions about what—or rather, all that—a schooling in the written word should be about. The measures of reading would vary from word accuracy to story engagement, from multiple-choice reading tests to videotapes of behaviors with books. The measures would include standardized reading scores, spelling accuracy, and technical and creative writing skills, as well as use of the library and an interest in writing careers. Automata Data would seek to ensure that studies be made available that compare these factors across programs at different ages, in different classrooms, among different students. It would provide samples of the work done by students. It would reveal how different combinations of the programs work, through both real instances and hypothetical modeling. It would consider recent alternative approaches, with research results pending.

A teacher or parent could turn to Automata Data to better understand what is known about reading among a given population of students, selected by age, or language background, or gender, or neighborhood. The Corporation's web site would reveal where the choice of a reading program does not appear to make any difference for children, as well as where it does, and how much difference it makes in test scores, reading attitudes, or other skills, over the short term or the long term. Automata Data would make clear to users that this knowledge does not dictate how best to teach this or that child, for its concerns are with organizing access to a comprehensible picture of what can be expected from a variety of approaches to reading instruction. It would also invite anyone using the site to comment on how the existing arrangement of research might be extended and made more useful for educators, parents, or researchers.

In this way, Automata Data would offer the public an education in what to expect from social science research. People would see that researchers disagree about what it means to sit down with a book, and how this can influence the way researchers go about gathering information and turning it into findings and recommendations. The research, then, is seen not as a way of finally deciding an issue, but as a way of participating in the decision-making process. This would perhaps transform the nature of public discourse, as the academic production of knowledge developed into far more of a public resource for those curious about and deeply engaged in different approaches to such questions as the teaching of reading.

I recognize that I am hardly alone in my concern over this need to bring greater order to what social science research brings to such issues. What Automata Data has to offer needs to be compared to what other efforts at greater coordination promise. For that reason, I offer here three other responses to the reading question, one commissioned by the U.S. government for public and professional consumption, and the other two organized by the reading research community for its own members. Each has something to teach about how we might better test the public usefulness and potential contribution social science research might make to our lives.

Professional Responses to the Reading Question

The U.S. federal government turns for advice on a variety of social and scientific issues to the distinguished National Academy of Sciences, commissioning blue-ribbon committees of scholars to assess the current state of knowledge and make recommendations. In this case, the Academy established a committee, led by Catherine Snow of Harvard, and including among others Barbara Foorman, to analyze the research literature and current programs on teaching reading. The committee published its report, *Preventing Reading Difficulties in Young Children*, in 1998. The committee's mandate bears a certain resemblance to what I intend for Automata Data:

> (1) To comprehend a rich but diverse research base; (2) to translate the research findings into advice and guidance for parents, educators, publishers, and others involved in the care and instruction of the young; (3) to convey this advice to the targeted audiences through a variety of publications, conferences, and other outreach activities.[13]

The National Academy of Sciences report makes only passing reference to the debate between phonics and whole language, noting that the controversy "has been persistent and heated, often obscuring the very real gains in knowledge of the reading process that have occurred."[14] Again, note the impatience with the diversity of perspectives on reading as opposed to the "very real gains in knowledge," presumably regarding the *true* nature of reading. If the report downplayed the sense of the debate, the *New York Times* chose to headline their lead front-page article on the Academy's report "Experts Call for Mix of 2 Methods To Teach Reading."[15] That mix turns out markedly in favor of phonics.

When it comes to what is to be done to prevent reading difficulties in young children, the report puts phonics first and foremost: "Beginning readers need explicit instruction and practice that leads to an appreciation that spoken words are made up of smaller units of sounds, familiarity with spelling-sound correspondences and common spelling conventions." Whole language is not without its place; the report allows that "fluency should be promoted through practice with a wide variety of well-written and engaging texts." There are also concessions made for "invented spellings," a favorite concept among whole-language teachers for encouraging students' pursuit of meaning and expression over accuracy, especially as, in the words of the report, allowing for such inventions "can be helpful for developing understanding of the identity and segmentation of speech sounds and sound-spelling relationships." The report does make it clear that direct instruction in phonics should only reflect a student's need for this skill. Yet when considering what makes a child into an independent reader, the report emphasizes "recognizing words primarily through attention to their letter-sound relationship."[16]

With its coverage of both approaches to reading, the National

Academy's report is undoubtedly a helpful synthesis of the research on reading, although Richard W. Riley, U.S. secretary of education, may be overstating it somewhat when he claims that "each of us can apply this report in our daily lives."[17] (I would not dare to have such ambitions for the daily utility of the whole of the social sciences through Automata Data.) This "translation" of the research, as the committee refers to its work, is still driven by a vision of a single best method, in a blended educational homogeneity. I can't help feeling that this selective synthesis, in itself, unnecessarily reduces the scope and value of what the research community has learned about the different ways of going about reading. The National Academy's expert panel sets up one group of researchers as arbiters not only of what research counts, but of what reading is best about, on behalf of public and practitioners.

On both political and epistemological grounds, I would prefer to offer the public the full context of debate and discrepancies within the research. It is important that public and practitioners, as well as researchers themselves, gain insight into how research on reading reflects the researchers' own understanding of reading, teaching, and the child. This is what I mean, in part, by making research more intelligible through a vehicle such as Automata Data. It also speaks to a larger educational process of helping the public to understand what to expect from the research.

When it comes to the researchers' best effort to date at finding the larger meaning of their field, we have what is known as the research handbook. In this case, the *Handbook of Reading Research* has a number of the field's leading scholars, describing what research in their specialty contributes to the study of reading, from word recognition to story comprehension.[18] The

Handbook runs to two volumes totaling two thousand pages, with the index listing the thousands of researchers cited in the work. These handbooks represent a major investment in making the field comprehensible to itself.

In the chapter on *word recognition*, for example, Keith Stanovich of Oakland University reviews various models of this "central sub-process of the complex act of reading." He carefully sets out how each model postulates a series of cognitive steps and components that are necessary for a reader to be able to recognize a word on a page. The research he describes has been focused on establishing how readers, in recognizing a word, grow less dependent on the text surrounding it as their reading skills develop, with Stanovich pointing out how these findings have stood the test of time.[19] He feels confident enough to conclude that the research on word recognition is "characterized by steady scientific progress," even as he acknowledges that "the most accurate model of the processing taking place within the word recognition module itself is, however, still a matter of serious dispute."[20]

I do not, however, wish to misrepresent the utility of this considerable research activity, for the *Handbook* also includes chapters on "teacher and school effects in learning to read," "teachers' instructional actions," and "comprehension instruction." These chapters, too, after exhausting reviews of the research literature, reflect a tone of hope and inspired energy for arriving at "more sophisticated answers" in the years to come, for achieving a greater focus on "helping teachers flexibly adapt their instructional actions to fit particular situations." The authors of these chapters identify "consistently successful strategies" in improving students' reading comprehension, such as drawing the students' attention to how a book is organized or making sure students connect new material to what they already know. But then the authors reviewing these strategies can also bring you up short, by daring to ask whether we should not compare how much students learn simply by reading to what they gain through direct instruction on reading.[21] Where does one point and click to affirm in these handbooks, yes, let's test that idea?

The *Handbook of Reading Research* concludes with an epilogue devoted to "understanding progress in reading research," by Peter Mosenthal of Syracuse University and Michael Kamil of Stanford University. Their chapter returns to an earlier print of mine, as Mosenthal and Kamil wrestle with both the very definition of *reading* and the related idea of what counts as progress in research on it. They quickly establish that amid all of this expertise, there is no consensus either on what reading is or on what the research has achieved. In response to this dilemma, they take a poststructural turn, following Michel Foucault, which leads them to divide researchers into two camps: those whose research is driven by the social and psychological problems associated with learning to read, and those who pursue the cognitive and neurological components that make up the act of reading. By the end of the epilogue, the best Mosenthal and Kamil can offer is to express their own earnest interest in learning which definition of reading and which model of research progress is best. The answer to such questions, they hold, could lead to a "basis for understanding the reading field."[22] I closed the book and sat for a moment over that rather less than rosy assessment of the field.

It is clearly troubling that so many reading researchers could be unable to arrive at a definition of something as basic as *reading*. However, the lesson here for an Automata Data is simply to give up on such ambitions, for a singular definition of a critical term is not a requirement of coherence for a body of knowledge. That reading means many things to many people need not be a deterrent to engaging teaching on language, effective lessons on decoding difficult words, or a wonderful time with a book or a screen. Recognizing the multiplicity of possibilities in ways of reading opens up opportunities for dialogue as much among researchers as among educators and the public. While I am sure some will worry that this smacks of a relativism that would allow the text in question to mean anything, I would counter that Automata Data will be very interested in researching the consequences and relationships among these ideas about reading. This information is intended to help people work together across a range of assumptions about what is most important about reading.

What researchers can offer through the public access of Automata Data on reading is a range of perspectives that may or may not speak to people's particular concerns over the reading done by their children, students, friends, neighbors, or employees. This range would help them ask questions about the standards by which reading and people are judged. It would permit them to see where and how different reading programs work, as well as the ends to which reading is directed. It would make that much more apparent to researchers where their work fits, in helping others find the pleasure and other benefits of reading, and where gaps remain in the analysis of learning to read. The scholars who take on the considerable job for Automata Data of making this body of work more intelligible and useful to a wider public would be recognized by their peers, and by the public, as making as great a contribution—I am daydreaming, perhaps—as might come from producing yet another study of reading. And it may be another daydream to assume that the effort at finding greater coherence within the diversity of approaches to reading would gradually influence how we go about research. Such is the inspiration that comes of sitting among the hefty handbooks of only the smallest portion of the social sciences.

As Automata Data would offer what is, in effect, a hyperlinked version of the literature review, I want to balance what has come before with a recent review of the research that strikes me as really working well at improving the public value of this inquiry into reading. "The Impending Demise of the Discrepancy Formula," by P. G. Aaron, published in the *Review of Educational Research*, may seem a strange exemplar for public knowledge, I realize.[23] Yet despite its unassuming title, it is nothing less than a methodical debunking of forty years of the much-ascribed Learning Disability (LD) syndrome, also known as dyslexia. While sweeping away much of the research literature on this topic, this study also manages to leave a real source of encouragement and hope in its place. That in itself is the kind of progress toward which Automata Data would be directed, even as it continues to provide a place for contrary research stances that support and oppose the value of the LD label.

Since it was first identified in the 1960s, LD has developed into a major educational industry devoted to helping children whose IQ scores seem well ahead of their reading scores. Aaron surveys approximately 180 studies, including large-scale meta-analyses of multiple studies, that lead him to believe that the Learning Disability label has not proven useful in diagnosing or teaching the students it was intended to help. This Indiana State University professor begins to dismantle the concept by calling into question the reliability of the two measures, the IQ score and the reading test score. But far more persuasive is the way he then brings forward a series of studies that demonstrate that (a) the poor reading of LD students resembles that of other poor readers, and (b) LD students respond much the same as other poor readers to similar reading lessons. He turns these findings into a source of hope for all students, by reviewing a range of studies that demonstrate the existence of decoding and comprehension strategies—such as helping students to become more aware of the purpose of reading—that improves the reading of all students. Along the way he points researchers to the "paucity of information about the degree of progress made during an academic year by poor readers," and to other reviews that "could not reach a firm conclusion because these studies, in addition to being flawed, yielded conflicting results."[24]

Aaron manages to offer something new and encouraging for researchers, practitioners, and parents. All that Automata Data would add to a contribution of this sort is a considerable boost in the potential circulation of this information (which at 20,000 copies for the *Review of Educational Research* is already high, for a research journal). Aaron's review is somewhat technical in places, with WRAT word-recognition performances and mean full-scale IQ scores, so that explanatory notes might be needed. Yet he concludes each section of his argument with effective summaries that, with perhaps the slightest touch, could serve most people interested in this question very well: "There is no convincing evidence to show that children with LD are qualitatively different from non-LD poor readers in terms of reading related cognitive processes, nor does differential placement and treatment appear to be more effective than leaving children with LD in the regular classroom."[25]

So what might happen if one came the Automata Data web site and searched under "dyslexia," "reading problems," or "Learning Disabilities"? It would lead to a general introduction to the topic, with Aaron's work listed among the available reviews of the research on this question. His work would first come up in summary form, with optional access to his more detailed analysis of the studies (as well as links to the studies and their data where possible). Given the controversial nature of his claims, there would inevitably be commentaries on Aaron's position, arranged in a similar fashion to permit drilling down into the details of the arguments, with links perhaps, in this case, to the responses of professional and parent associations (which have no small stake in this particular topic). The question of what studies need to follow from this review of LD would form a special category for discussion among researchers, joined perhaps by concerned members of the public and government agencies. Aaron would be invited to update his review after a period of time, and to respond to criticisms of it as well as to more supportive reviews of LD research. People would know, on entering Automata Data to learn more about the topic, that they will able to consult a variety of opinions and the evidence each calls upon, while retaining responsibility for making up their own minds about what to do in light of this knowledge.

My case for Automata Data, then, is relatively straightforward. Let us use these new information technologies to create public access to the whole of social science inquiry, to the differences of opinion and the range of interests, which are but extensions of public opinion in scholarly guise. Let us turn away from blue-ribbon committees that seek to reassure the public that the social sciences have made real strides toward authoritative, objective and singular truths on any given issue. The social sciences, when they are done well, are no less a part of public knowledge and its ensuing debates over what matters most. There is little point in pretending otherwise in exchange for some small measure of scientific or professional status.

The social sciences need to be a greater part of the democratic articulation, elaboration, debate, and extension of ideas about how we are to live. There is nothing impartial in the researcher's feeling for what reading is all about or for any other aspect of human life. The social sciences are but one manner of testing claims, realizing consequences, and identifying risks and possibilities. Increasing the researcher's public participation, not as outside expert invited to pronounce recommendations, but as a cross between public utility and community activist, has become for me a focal point for renewing the social contract that has long held between the social sciences and the public.

5

....

Social Contract

THE SOCIAL SCIENCES are not the only disciplines currently weathering a loss, if not a crisis, in public confidence. In fact, when it comes to public-funding cuts, the social sciences seem blessedly out of sight and mind. They have been spared the steady decline in support suffered (at least until very recently) by the National Endowment for the Humanities, and they have not felt the project-killing cuts experienced by "big science" supercolliders and other ventures.[1] The social sciences have been only lightly scarred by the exposés launched by such works as *ProfScam* and *Tenured Radicals* against seemingly scandalous academic sinecures.[2] So, why not leave well enough alone?

I risk dwelling on the public value of social science research not only because something needs to done, but because I believe something *can* be done at this point, to renew the good faith that originally underwrote the social sciences' contract with society at large. Better this renewal should come from within, at a time when the social sciences are not under direct assault. Better it should come while the vast new information networks are still in their formative years, when some part of them can still be shaped, perhaps, by public interests.

The social sciences have no special claim to serving humanity within the university. What could be said to set them apart from other academic disciplines is that their study of humanity might have wider public appeal and interest than the classics or particle physics. The social sciences offer forms of knowledge that might be thought useful to people, useful within the personal and political scope of their lives. In addition, the social sciences also bear, along with other academic disciplines, responsibility for knowledge that serves an array of related professional fields such as education, justice, health, welfare, government, and social organizations generally.[3] These twin elements of public and professional service constitute the basis of the social contract the social sciences have struck with the larger society.

Jean-Jacques Rousseau, who did much to make the social contract a foundation of democracy, insists at the very opening of his book on the subject that such a concept was necessary "in order that justice and utility may in no case be divided."[4] Such is my concern. Can we do a better job of bringing justice and utility together in what the social sciences' might offer to the public? The question has haunted the social sciences since their beginning. In 1825, when Henri Saint-Simon published his plans for improving France's social institutions, he called for "scientific research which sought to establish a new political theory . . . [that] would as far as possible direct the people's work toward the improvement of their moral and physical existence."[5]

For nearly two centuries now, the implied social contract between those who study society and those who are studied has been variously worked and phrased. Although I am no lawyer, I imagine the wording of this implied contract between the social sciences and the public to go something like this: "In exchange for supporting social science research, you will be the beneficiary of untold knowledge directed at helping improve, shall we say after Saint-Simon, your moral and physical existence."

With this statement, I have been careful to capture one of the lingering and troubling ambiguities for the social sciences. Read it again, and note how difficult it is to determine who this knowledge is directed at or who is to possess and use this knowledge. That is, it is not always clear whether the knowledge promised by the social sciences is intended for both public and professional consumption. Listen to the ambiguity in the claims of sociologists Daniel Lerner, who speaks of sociology's "democratic commitment: knowledge for betterment," and Charles Lemert, who holds that his discipline serves "all individuals desiring to come to some workable terms with the world."[6] For whom does this knowledge toll, when it claims to toll for the betterment of us all?

For me, what makes the contract democratic, what brings justice and utility together, is the assurance that the professional knowledge of the social sciences is finding its way into the hands and minds of the people, when it can be shown that this knowing helps people make sense, pose questions, raise challenges, find wonder, change minds, and take action. The *public* value of the social sciences I am promoting here through Automata Data —and I realize that not all social science research claims to be of public value—lies in its contributions to public knowledge, whether that means coming "to some workable terms with the world" or against the world. This is radically different from asking the public to trust that this professional knowledge will be used on their behalf. This risks excluding the public as a party to the social contract between the social sciences and the state, undermining its democratic basis.

In the past—before the info-deluge, we might say—the social sciences also assumed a responsibility for organizing their contributions to knowledge in a publicly comprehensible way, as if the simple generation of new knowledge could not fulfill this social contract in good faith. Auguste Comte, founding visionary and eventual lunatic mystic of the social sciences, described the need for a "social physics" (for which he also coined the term *sociology*) that would complete "the system of natural sciences." As such, this unity of knowledge would "determine and maintain a complete mental coherence such as never before existed even in the best ordered and most advanced minds."[7] This coherence in understanding human development could only be achieved, he foresaw in 1830, if supported by a "distinct class of men . . . whose special and permanent function would consist in connecting each new special discovery with the general system."[8] He foresaw the need to find the order to what was known, in a tension that he identified between consolidation and progress. And while the social sciences have since rejected, in large measure, the model of physics, the field is still in need of greater "mental coherence" and connections to each new special discovery. The "special and permanent function" of an Automata Data, after all, would be to offer people a more coherent and connected picture of the social sciences' enormous range of activity, in all of its different forms of understandings and approaches to knowledge.

This theme of coherence and connection returns some time after Comte introduced it, with the formation of the American Social Science Association in 1865. This nonacademic group of intellectuals and reformers made sure that their Association not only contributed to the welfare of society, but shouldered its responsibility for establishing a common ground of understanding:

Its objects [the Association set out] are to aid the development of Social Science, and to guide the public mind to the best practical means of promoting the Amendment of Laws, the Advancement of Education, the Prevention and Repression of Crime, the Reformation of Criminals, and the Progress of Public Morality, the adoption of Sanitary Regulations, and the diffusion of principles on questions of Economy, trade and Finance. It will give attention to Pauperism, and the topics related thereto including the responsibility of the well-endowed and successful, the wise and the educated, to the honest and respectable, for the failures of others. It will aim to bring together the various societies and individuals now interested in these objects, for the purpose of obtaining by discussion the real elements of Truth; by which doubts are removed, conflicting opinions harmonized, and a common ground afforded for treating wisely the great social problems of the day.[9]

By the turn of the century, the do-gooder clubbishness of the ASSA, along with its pursuit of a common ground, forcibly harmonized, gave way to the academic specializations that took root in the modern university. There were scholarly careers to be made within the departmental divisions of anthropology, economics, history, political science, psychology, sociology, and statistics, each determined to set off its own proper domain of study replete with scholarly and scientific methods, some original, others borrowed. Still, that initial impulse, concerned with directing knowledge toward amending, advancing, preventing, and reforming the social realm, was not to be shaken. The social sciences continue to be driven by this double force of social benefit and scholarly aspiration.[10]

It was not long before the particular costs of specialization—largely, as I have already suggested, in the coherence and coordination that could be brought to the analysis of social issues—became all too apparent. Departmental divisions among the disciplines of the social sciences were seen to stand in the way of more complete and comprehensive analyses of social problems, and in 1923 the Social Science Research Council was formed to remedy the problem. The Council committed itself to working against fragmentation-by-specialization, largely by organizing through its membership a more coherent approach to major research questions. To this day, the Council continues to conduct broad interdisciplinary studies for the government and other agencies. In the words of its current president, Kenneth Prewitt, the Council searches for "a more continuous and integrated knowledge" in its efforts to "add to the sum total of human happiness and welfare."[11]

Well after the Social Science Research Council was established, the sociologist Robert Lynd, perhaps best known for his classic study of small-town America, *Middleton*, tried to come to terms with a similar crisis of confidence in the social sciences with his strikingly titled *Knowledge for What?*[12] Some questions have a way of persisting.

Lynd called the social sciences to task on their tired claim that they did not have enough data to arrive at a firm answer to much of anything. He shot back that when it came to data, there was all too much of the stuff. The problem, as he saw it, was that the data were only used to produce further descriptions of the social situation. What was needed was some way of advancing the true goals of the social sciences, which he identified as *prediction* and *control*. Knowledge, it seemed obvious to him in the 1930s, enabled an ordering of the world that could render it manageable in ways that could secure our happiness within it.

Lynd demands that sociology face up to its failure to do enough to resolve the world's social problems. He holds the social sciences responsible for a "desperate betrayal indeed."[13] He dares to wonder how his colleagues can blithely go on teaching courses and supervising dissertations, "without the question ever being raised as to what is to be done with all this knowledge." What have they done, he asks, "other than to give more lectures and to supervise the writing of more dissertations?" He then goes on to question "what do human beings want this particular institutional-complex [of the university] to do for us, what is the most direct way to do it, and what do we need in order to do it?"[14]

While I am drawn to his forceful questioning of his profession, especially his interest in what people want to know, Lynd and I go our very different ways in responding to these concerns. He leans toward social engineering, through "a large and pervasive extension of planning and control to many areas now left to individual initiative."[15] The renewal of the social contract I am proposing entails the engineering of knowledge, not people. The public access to the knowledge afforded by the social sciences is intended to inform, if not inspire, both individual and collective initiatives. And ready public access to this knowledge may well be useful for interrupting Lyndian extensions of planning and control.

This brings me to a distinction made in the social sciences between *applied, policy,* or *technical* research and research that is not directly involved in evaluating or otherwise addressing programs or policies.[16] Lynd's call for action was a call for applied research that would help particular institutional-complexes do things for us. The great era of applied social science took place between Lyndon Johnson's declaration of "unconditional war on poverty" in 1964 and Ronald Reagan's election in 1980. The times were such that government corridors were thick with economists and program evaluation specialists working directly on policy initiatives. What brought the era to an end, at least in the estimation of Princeton sociologist Robert Nathan, is the social scientists' failure to bring in sufficient good news for the programs' champions in government. Social scientists, rigorous researchers that they were, proved more adept at identifying the problems and ironies of the new programs than at coming up with solutions that produced unequivocally successful results.[17]

While an Automata Data would obviously provide a thorough guide to the realm of applied research and its limits, it would do so within the context of its larger concern with finding better ways of informing public discussion, better ways of creating a public resource. This would not preclude governments or other agencies commisioning Automata Data to coordinate a range of studies directed at shaping policy and programs, but it would also ensure that the research would be part of the public record.[18] But by the same token Automata Data would do well to link up theoretical studies and invite commentaries that spoke to the limits of knowledge, the history of ideas, and other topics that go beyond research news you can use. The public interest in the larger questions—the *Brief History of Time* syndrome, we might call it, after the enormous public success of Stephen Hawking's demanding tour of cosmology and astrophysics—should not be underestimated.

The public has a right to all that the social sciences are making of the world, if only because that pursuit of knowledge is being conducted as a public trust. The results of this research may inform and unsettle debates on policy and programs; it may equip those prepared to bite the hands of bureaucrats and other authorities who assume that they alone have the expertise to engineer social practices. For this call to public service is not about

forcing or shaming the social sciences into the "illiberal practicality" of bureaucratic servitude, as the sociologist C. Wright
Mills identified the danger in the late 1950s.

Mills was appalled by the social sciences' eager pursuit of contract research, so ready to "serve whatever ends its bureaucratic
clients may have in view." The social scientist was in danger of
playing the engineer of human souls rather than the informant
of public debate. This toadying would only result, Mills warned,
in making "authority more effective and more efficient by providing information of use to authoritative planners."[19] These are
not the goals of an Automata Data. The renewal of the social contract I am proposing between public and social sciences is about
furthering, and learning more about, knowledge's service to democracy.

Today, however, when it comes to public engagement the social
sciences are more often accused of playing partisan politics than
of succumbing to bureaucratic servitude. William Epstein, in the
School of Social Work at the University of Nevada, presents a co-
gent analysis of how the social sciences got caught up in liberal
and conservative agendas for the most recent round of welfare
reform, which led to the Personal Responsibility and Work Opportunity Reconciliation Act of 1996. He has subtitled his book
"How Social Science Fails the Poor," and the culprit he identifies
is just this partisan mix of advocacy and research.[20] Among the
political forces at work on this issue, the conservative attacks and
liberal defenses of welfare each have their corresponding lines
of research that feed their respective rhetoric with facts, figures,
and arguments.

The conservative research agenda pursues character and family structure, as well as the effectiveness of workfare and private
charity. They also look for evidence of the liberal welfare state's

failings, especially as it sanctions the rejection of personal responsibility.[21] Liberal proposals for universal entitlement, on the other hand, are supported by evaluation studies of job training and placement services and of mental health and social support programs.[22] This amounts to two distinct research programs. And for Epstein, it is bad science conducted at the expense of the poor and the effectiveness of the social policies. Epstein argues that the social sciences should dedicate themselves to securing "objective and reliable information for public discussion of social problems" principally on the initial and sustaining causes for poverty.[23]

On the other hand, my support for introducing social science research into public discussion, including knowledge of what brings about poverty, does not depend on a belief that the pursuit of objectivity will redeem the political function of the research and its partiality. As I insisted in the case of reading research, the pursuit of knowledge takes many forms in the hands of engaged and rigorous researchers, and those forms are shaped in part by the researchers' values. The partiality of social science research, especially if it is clarified and made explicit, as Epstein helpfully does, can become a very helpful resource for public discussion of the issues, without shutting it down under the guise of making objective pronouncements on, say, the *real* causes of poverty.

To put it another way, I would fear an irrefutably authoritative social science, if I thought such a thing were possible. The social sciences are simply not going to succeed at playing referee or umpire for ideological disputes over social issues, as some have suggested.[24] They can make available to those caught up in the disputes greater empirical understanding of what is at issue, as well as, one hopes, a more profound and systematic level of inquiry.

Given how researchers on aspects of welfare are divided, Automata Data would strive, much as many journals do today, to provide as fair a forum as possible for the range of stances in the research, while also making an effort to help the public consulting this research to see the assumptions which divide these positions. Automata Data would support the development of common measures across studies, perhaps for assessing equality levels, social harmony, and civic participation. This would improve the opportunities for comparing claims and results, while supporting alternative readings of the data. Minds may not be changed, but the consequences of positions taken may well be better understood and appreciated.

By juxtaposing contrasting studies on welfare and making apparent the fundamental differences in orientation and interests, Automata Data will help people to see that there can be no pretense of an objective approach to questions of poverty and civic responsibility. Nor is Automata Data likely to achieve a perfect balance in its representation of partisan approaches. At best, the always partial work of the social sciences would expand and enrich that otherwise shrinking public space for working through such questions in more than sound-bite segments. This duty— to make the knowledge that we in the social sciences are otherwise so busy producing more easily and readily available—will weigh heavily on what follows, as I ask in the remainder of this chapter what within our sources of support and sense of professional autonomy speaks to this social contract, this democratic obligation.

Research Investment

Two centuries ago, before the Founding Fathers had completed what would become the Constitution, the Northwest Ordinance of 1787 had already affirmed the critical role of knowledge in this new American democracy: "Knowledge, being necessary to good government and the happiness of mankind, schools and means of education, shall forever be encouraged."[25] The federal government has seen to the encouragement and support of that knowledge in a variety of ways, most notably today in the social sciences with the Social, Behavioral, Economic Sciences (SBE) division of the National Science Foundation (NSF). The SBE defines its research mission as seeking "to improve understanding of human beings, their many activities, and the organizations they create." It uses the language of public investment: "There is consensus among economists and policy researchers that public investments in science and engineering yield very high annual rates of return to society. Furthermore, the activities supported by NSF—fundamental research and education based at academic institutions—are generally viewed as among the most productive of all Federal investments."[26]

This theme of public good runs like a river through all that the National Science Foundation would claim on behalf of the research it sponsors, whether in the social or in the pure sciences:

> By enabling leadership across the frontiers of science and engineering, NSF's investments bolster the nation's quality of life and standard of living. As noted economist Paul Romer said in a recent comment on the roots of economic growth, "If we didn't keep finding new ideas, there really would be limits to growth. It's ideas—the whole process of discovery—that cause growth."

Here is the earnest attempt to root the social contract in a knowledge economy that is dependent on the government's research investment. And in some ways, I envision Automata Data testing this hypothesis that, in the case of the social sciences, this knowledge bolsters the nation's quality of life, if not its standard of living, by doing much more to ensure that this understanding of personal and public processes is more widely and publicly available.

The Social, Behavioral, Economic Sciences division of the NSF supports a wide range of social science activity, with a declared bias toward work "based on empirical observation or . . . subject to empirical validation."[27] In addition, the SBE intervenes in the free marketplace of ideas by establishing special programs to support particular policy initiatives, for example on gender equity in the sciences. SBE projects that advance "our understanding of social processes and social structures" range from the development of Geographical Information Systems—which can aid market research, real estate developments, and emergency responses—to studies of how Balinese Water Temples manage complex irrigation systems.[28] It may seem just plain vulgar to put dollar figures on such work, as if to cost out the public trust factor in this social contract. But given how politically vulnerable the monies are, with budgets being cut in many areas, I am making my appeal not only to the sense of responsibility, but to the self-interest of those in the social sciences. In 1997, the SBE division of the NSF had a budget of $130 million out of the NSF's total of roughly $3.4 billion.[29]

One might wonder what small part on a billion-dollar B-2 stealth bomber is represented by this investment in the public good, but the relative size of the social science support is not going to protect it from public challenges and budget cuts, if what the social sciences produce is seen as minuscule and of dubious value outside its own immediate realm. We might heed the warning posed by Jules Feiffer, who, in one of his op-art cartoons, has a reactionary character respond to federal funding for the arts with the question "Why should I give my tax dollar to what makes me feel like a jerk?"[30] If anything, the social sciences are under a greater compulsion than the arts to offer some sensible return on the tax-dollar investment. Can social scientists afford to make their work a little more accommodating and accessible without feeling they have soiled and sold their souls? In this way, what I am proposing through Automata Data raises critical issues affecting both research ethics and academic freedom. I want to argue for expanding those ethics to encompass greater public responsibility in ways that serve, perhaps surprisingly to some, at least one strong reading of academic freedom.

Research Ethos and Ethics

The insularity of social science research is not going to cut it under the renewed social contract between profession and public I am advocating here. Research produced for other researchers, and for those whom they teach, falls short of what I am suggesting is the presumed and funded contract underwriting the social sciences. Despite grant-winning prose to the contrary from social scientists, the profession tends toward trickle-down informatics, in the belief that some part of this wealth of knowledge will make its way into the public domain. Even where it makes a major concession to the public—as in the case of research ethics—social science research does little to realize its obligation toward the public value of the knowledge so rigorously pursued. The adoption over the last few decades of a very strong program of research ethics has become a way of wrapping this public responsibility in form letters and checklists. The elaborate set of procedures designed to protect those who serve as subjects in research studies may seem to absolve the social sciences of further obligation. This profession is then quit of any further *ethical* responsibilities for this knowledge, once those who have donated some aspect of their lives to its creation have been treated fairly.

What goes missing is any consideration of the public's access rights, as a whole, to the information they have underwritten in the belief that it was in their best interests. Practitioners in a number of fields have magazines, such as *Educational Leadership*, that make the results of research readily available, and there are a few newsstand titles, such as Transaction's *Society*, that do the same, on a broader basis. But as I have tried to make clear, the public does not have a readily accessible and permanent source for uncovering what the social sciences have been able to learn on a given topic, apart from those communities that house a good university library and those people who have the time and skills to use it.

Lest you find this statement on the narrowly professional focus of social science research ethos and ethics extreme, let me offer the evidence of two distinguished guides to social science research. My first exhibit is one of the profession's substantial how-to books: *Research Methods in the Social Sciences* by Chava Frankfort-Nachmias and David Nachmias, of the University of Wisconsin at Madison, now into its fifth edition.[31] The book's approach to choosing a topic illustrates how the social sciences could do far more to secure the connections between public and research interests.

The relevant chapter opens this way: "In the beginning is the problem." It suggests that time and world begin with the problem in hand. Failing that, the authors allow that "the best source for stimulating the statement of problems and hypothesis is the professional literature."[32] On the other hand, it now seems painfully obvious to me that the research has to begin with a consideration of how the public will gain by this knowledge, both by what it adds to the overall coherence of existing work and by how it speaks to current understandings.[33]

Automata Data would be concerned with helping public and researchers develop research topics that grow out of a two-way educational process concerned with establishing just what social sciences can contribute to public discourse. While a body of "outreach scholarship" has emerged that is directed at serving specific communities, there can be varying degrees of community participation and consultation that an Automata Data could support.[34] This interest in service need not diminish the impetus of what we might call the ethics of disruptive research that is intended to confront what the community refuses or denies. Such initiatives are no less driven by the need to augment public knowledge. And then there is the fact that Automata Data is not intended to encompass all that is done in the name of social science scholarship, but only that part of it that claims to be in the public interest.

Among those who would support this greater accountability in the formation of social science research projects is Rogers Smith, a political scientist at Yale, who tempers the free and rigorous pursuit of all matters political by calling for "special attention to those [topics or problems] that are predictably neglected, for both intellectual and political reasons, by governmental and private-sector analysts, politicians, and the media."[35] Smith exhorts the profession to pursue questions people care about, to work with what people "experience as problems" but lack the skills (and I would add the privileged position of professorial work) to explore. He makes no bones about the importance of going after the hard and sometimes "impolitic" questions that arise from pursuing public concerns: "I cannot think of a different sense of disciplinary purpose that would be as likely to contribute important knowledge about politics that people would not get elsewhere, at least not in as careful or rigorous a form." This is, for Smith, "about as scientific and as serviceable to democracy as we can honestly get."[36] Although he pays little enough attention to how best to bring this knowledge to the public, he at least observes how the technical specialization of political science—with its talk of strategically rational goal-maximizing behaviors within institutional matrices—can lead citizens "to decide that politics *is* beyond them."[37]

When it comes to explicitly addressing the research ethics of the social sciences, Frankfort-Nachmias and Nachmias hold in *Research Methods in the Social Sciences* that "ethical issues arise from the kinds of problems social scientists investigate and the methods used to obtain valid and reliable data." They then offer a considerable list of ethical challenges, which does an excellent job of setting out the current ethical boundaries of research in the social sciences:

> [Ethical issues] may be evoked by the research problem itself (e.g., genetic engineering, determinants of intelligence, program evaluation), the setting in which the research takes place (hospitals, prisons, public schools, government agencies), the procedures required by the research design (exposure of the experimental group to conditions that might have effects on the participants), the method of data collection (covert participant observation), the kinds of per-

sons serving as research participants (the poor, children, people with AIDS, politicians), and the type of data collected (personal information, recruitment practices in public agencies).[38]

These ethical issues are focused on the immediate impact of the research on the research subject or program rather than on a larger ethics of what responsibilities are entailed in seeking knowledge in the name of some greater public good. Even the genetic engineering reference, which is a caution over the impact of the research on the world, carries no greater social obligation than to take into account the damage that might be done, if things were to go awry.

This chapter also includes "A Code of Ethics for Social Scientists," developed by Paul Davidson Reynolds as a composite of twenty-four codes he assembled from various universities. Reynolds's list does specify that research reports should be made freely available along with their sources of funding. But for me the ethical question also falls between what is freely available and what is publicly intelligible, especially as it adds to the coherence of the research venture in all its diversity. The list does not mention ethical concerns with the research's contribution to public or practitioner.[39] Missing from this ethical code is the sense of the larger public sponsorship and trust that might be entailed in this social contract between researcher and society.

What is presumed to drive this quest for knowledge is the researcher's autonomy as a professional, in an ethics of interest that is most commonly suggested by how often researchers say, "what interests me is . . ." Frankfort-Nachmias and Nachmias speak of "the responsibility of the scientist" without addressing its relationship to the knowledge sought and how it might serve others.

I am not suggesting that the research that comes out of this ethos lacks accountability or is irresponsible. It is bound to be peer-reviewed at every stage, from the grant proposal to its selection for publication, but those blind and disinterested peers share this ethos that is generally unconcerned with the larger public value of the work. And the questions of academic freedom, which I am so clearly begging, will be taken up below, after I offer a second opinion on the scope of professional responsibility.

While a Fellow at the Woodrow Wilson International Center for Scholars in Washington, D.C., the sociologist Gary Marx found the time to publish thirty-seven "moral imperatives" for his aspiring colleagues.[40] His prescription of "methods and manners" was inspired by a desire to prevent "many a mid-life crisis" by sharing what had worked for him.[41] He rightly admonishes social scientists to write clearly and think critically. He questionably advises them to write books, rather than read them. He is more suggestive in asking that research be problem-focused, and that it speak truth to power. He asks that researchers recognize those times when they are "operating as a scientist" and when as "a more explicit political actor."[42] Marx playfully admonishes his colleagues to have fun and a sense of humor, which I would welcome, too, and yet I am less comfortable with his strictures to "have a fresh argument" and "write everywhere, all the time, on everything." This absence of purpose, beyond production, may be more telling of the profession than Marx realizes, with its image of social scientists simply seeking to fill up the spaces, hoping against hope that something will come of it all. Is there not some greater purpose or urgency to this calling, one wants to ask? The question leads to Marx's longest and final moral imperative.

It begins elliptically with, "Keep the faith! . . ." It is a faith that he then goes on to describe as a belief "that empirical and scientific knowledge about human and social conditions can result in the improvement of those conditions."[43] How is it that this improvement is an act of faith, rather than the very focus on our efforts? How is it that the social sciences are not focusing more of their energies on creating moral imperatives and research strategies directed at ensuring the basis of that improvement? "Take it on faith" seems to me an inadequate basis for building a research enterprise. Automata Data is all about testing one aspect of that faith, namely that the knowledge acquired in the name of the social sciences contributes to people's efforts at comprehending and enacting improvements. It calls for an expanded research ethics and ethos that sees itself far more highly tuned to public interests and to making the resulting knowledge into a public resource. But how can I put off any longer the question of whether this will so unduly compromise academic freedom that our very hopes for knowledge will be dashed?

Academic Freedom

However much is written of the social sciences' ameliorative force on social ills, many social scientists believe that what keeps their practice honest, pure, and free of politics is how little they owe the world, outside of professional and disciplinary structures. This scholarly dedication to professional autonomy ensures that our research practices are directed, often in a Kafkaesque fashion, at pleasing the "blind" gatekeepers of the castle-like state of the profession. This review process takes little more than a passing interest in how an individual researcher's progress relates to the public value of the profession's knowledge as a whole.

I can perhaps best frame this issue of autonomy through caricature and contrast. Given that I have composed this book while serving as a visiting professor at Seattle University in a Chair endowed by the Boeing Company, I can imagine a chain of assumptions underwriting social science practices that goes something like this: *The social science quest for knowledge is not like engineering an airplane. Social scientists are not designing the parts of a plane, with an eye to how it all fits together within the required specs of time, cost, and safety. What a thought! Where is the academic freedom in that, the intellectual creativity? We must be trusted to throw light on whatever interests us, whatever draws support. We certainly build on the work of others, always properly citing what we borrow. But we do not plan our work like an engineer designing a wing to fit snugly with a certain fuselage. We are far more the intellectual, the artist even, than the engineer. Yet like the engineer, we build what we believe will help humankind, if only in ways that may not fly within our lifetimes.*[44]

If this overstates academic autonomy, it does so in the face of a public that has learned not to count on the social sciences for guidance on bilingual education, learning to read, or improving academic performance generally. The National Academy of Education committee that examined the research agenda on bilingual education, which I cited earlier, points out that "if there are two issues that make education researchers and research administrators grimace, it is coordination of research efforts and dissemination of results—not because they do not want to do these things, but because no one seems to have clear answers about effective ways of doing them."[45]

Fortunately, there are encouraging exceptions. Certainly, the social sciences proved decisive in convincing a great number of people in the 1960s of smoking's dangers, when biological explanations of the cause and effect between lung cancer and cigarettes were not available. The social sciences also sharpened the public's perception of just how serious gender and racial inequities were in the workplace and other arenas. But clearly much more could be done to serve public interests, given the amount of research activity going on in the social sciences.

Yet it is undoubtedly fair to ask whether such service means an end to the treasured concept of academic freedom and an encouragement of anti-intellectualism. As I understand and appreciate the concept, academic freedom protects the scholar's work from undue outside interference. The research is guided by the search for the truth wherever it leads. This ensures that it need not win a popularity contest or survive a democratic vote to proceed. Almost. Research is repeatedly subjected to the balloting of a peer-review process from within a profession that is far from perfect. Consider the instructive example of feminist literary critics, who initially ran afoul of their peers (and continue to do so) in their pursuit of a scholarship in which they felt compelled to address the decidedly public problem of patriarchal structures. Academic freedom failed them a number of times in those early days, but the problem in that case was not public interference, but interference from their colleagues. The current system can certainly protect the public's interests insofar as peers alone possess the competence to advise and judge certain qualities of the work.[46] And I imagine that research posted by Automata Data would continue to be governed by this review process, if somewhat more inspired by a commitment to increase the public contribution and intelligibility of the work. Its stance on academic freedom would not then disturb even the obviously concerned Herbert London, professor of humanities at New York Univer-

sity. London recently called for a redefinition of academic freedom, so that "propagandizing on behalf of one's favorite cause
[apart from say academic freedom] should be discouraged unless
it can be demonstrated that such an appeal is consistent with the
canons of scholarship."[47]

In 1915, the then recently formed American Association of University Professors addressed this relationship between public and
profession by holding up the university as an "intellectual experiment station" that offered an "inviolable refuge" from the forces
of public opinion and political authority. At the same time, the
Association determined that "the responsibility of the university
teacher is to the public itself, and to the judgment of his [sic] own
profession."[48] I would add that this responsibility, given the educational aspect of university positions, entails leadership in finding ways of realizing that responsibility to the public itself. The
knowledge that comes from this experiment station can be cast
as both a service for and a force on the public. At this point, however, academic knowledge reaches the public, as I've noted, most
often through the sound-bites of talking heads. These brief media spots hardly do justice to the craft and contribution research
might otherwise bring to bear for those among the public who
really want to see what the social sciences have assembled in the
name of knowledge.

Among contemporary discussions of academic freedom, I
would hold with Richard Rorty's standard of assessing it in light
of the "good which these universities do, to their role in keeping
democratic government and liberal institutions alive and functioning."[49] This Stanford University philosopher is blunt about
the need to shift away from "an epistemological justification for
academic freedom," which can set the disinterested purity of

knowledge against expressions of public interests. Rorty also offers the caution that "neither philosophers nor anyone else can offer us nice sharp distinctions between appropriate social utility and inappropriate politicization." He insists that the inevitable debate over such distinctions is the very work of the university, if it is to remain "healthy and free."[50] Automata Data would, of course, only raise the profile of such distinctions and debate, because the results for the social sciences would be within easy reach of the public.

As for the social sciences, Rorty proposes that "sociologists and psychologists might stop asking themselves whether they are following rigorous scientific procedures and start asking themselves whether they have any suggestions to make to their fellow citizens about how our lives, or our institutions, should be changed."[51] Rorty ultimately turns to John Dewey's pragmatic sense of truth to establish what this academic freedom is devoted to accomplishing: for this is about a truth that "clears up difficulties," Dewey writes, "removes obscurities, puts individuals into more experimental, less dogmatic, and less arbitrarily skeptical relation to life."[52]

As it now stands, the social sciences have it within their reach, if not completely within their ethos, to do a far better job of clearing up difficulties and obscurities. This clarity might diminish people's skepticism not only about the world around them but about what the social sciences have to offer the world. Although Rorty tends to favor the poet and novelist over the social scientist (and philosopher) as inspirations for social advancement, he can clearly serve as an inspirational figure for projects such as mine.

Typically, when it comes to discussions of academic freedom, scholars are quick to reach for John Stuart Mill's credo that the truth emerges from the unimpeded and free marketplace of ideas. The economic analogy has grown a little shopworn, as the university proves a highly subsidized marketplace in which the circulation of ideas is principally restricted to other producers, that is, suppliers creating their own demands. Meanwhile government and private granting agencies exert their own market pressure through special funding initiatives and other sorts of targeted programs. But then I suppose the actual marketplace, on which this metaphor is based, has become increasingly focused on mergers and acquisitions intended to limit the market, while developing universal platforms and industry-wide standards and consolidation on a global basis that Automata Data only seeks to imitate on behalf of public knowledge interests.

Having said this much on the renewed social contract I envision, I hope I have also made it clear that I am aware of how perverse, how near-Stalinist it must seem to propose that the social sciences consider central planning or engineering models for coordinating the analysis of social dilemmas. I have only turned to this corporate response because I despair at any other means of producing a coherent body of information of value to a public facing increasingly complex social problems without a dedicated guide to the efforts of thousands and thousands of social science researchers.

Metaphorically speaking, all the parts of the social science airplane are designed and produced independently, with some areas of the plane well attended to and others ignored, with prospective passengers asked not only to decide among competing designs, but to fit them together before departing. Yet while speaking of business, I also have to ask why it is that those who play the stock market or, for that matter, watch sports have remarkably complete and coherent data sets available to them.

The information does not render the world predictable—

where's the play in that?—but like the commentaries on it, it does help people feel like they are on top of the game, as informed and aware as they could hope to be, with the actual calls left to their wits.[53] It doesn't take a grand theory of social formations and relations. It doesn't rely on a single method or a consensus over results. But the generation of this information is very clearly focused on feeding a public desire to know. And if stocks and sports are neatly contained universes compared to the issues that trouble the social sciences, this fact does not preclude following us or John Stuart Mill in borrowing from that other marketplace.

If we were to take a lesson from the brokerage house, it might be from Charles Schwab & Co., whose motto is *Information. Access. Control.*™ Schwab recently ran a full-page advertisement in newspapers describing the advantages of buying stock using their new online service over going the typical route of a full-commission broker.[54] The ad uses a flow chart showing two possible paths for an investor. One path begins with a call to the full-commission broker, and the other with logging onto www.schwab.com. In the first branch of the chart, the investor first plays phone-tag, before engaging the broker in a discussion in which "Investor asks for 100 shares of stock A," and is met by "Broker suggests 100 shares of stock B." After this is repeated, "Investor asks to see stock B's five-year history," followed by "Broker says *he's* seen it." Next, "investor asks to see detailed report of company," to which "broker says don't worry." Then "investor asks for a real-time quote" and "broker says he'll call right back," at which point "broker goes for lunch." Get the picture? Then there is the other path. The investor logs onto the Schwab web site. The web site offers three online information services: Dow Jones, which presents "news on a specific stock"; Standard and

Poor's, which presents "in-depth company report"; and Big Charts, which presents comparisons of a "stock's historical process to its moving average." Having consulted these informative sources, the investor "places order for 100 shares at market."

While the ad makes the point that the online service takes only fifteen minutes, compared to seven hours of broker-chasing, time is not what is at issue—for me, at least. What stands out in the context of my project is how the web site changes the relationship between client and information. The client has information, access, and control, to put it in terms of Schwab's motto; or better yet, the client has direct *access* to a greater array of *information*, which assures greater *control*. The personal client-broker relationship is lost, it is true, but that is far less an issue between social scientist and public. Schwab is using the web to allow its clients more direct participation in this knowledge economy. The Schwab client, and eventually the Automata Data client as well, will require an understanding of how this information is organized; given the latter's role in democratic decision making, training in its use might form part of a civics education.

The financial industry is currently supported by a $6.5 billion information-services industry. The social sciences run one at considerably less investment, but their version has not really been tested in terms of the support it might provide for the vast social enterprise of the public sector. Instead of a financial investor looking to buy 100 shares, clients for the social sciences' information services include schools selecting reading programs; parents wishing to compare treatments for an ill child; voters facing an Official English proposition on a ballot; a community working through a flare-up of racial tensions; city officials reviewing urban renewal proposals; reporters writing about the drop in crime; an environmentalist group developing educational programs; and a government agency preparing a policy on services for immigrants.

If members of these various groups logged onto an Automata Data, they would be able to establish what the social sciences have to offer, as well as pose questions to databases of relevant statistics, query the history of responses to the phenomenon, review interviews of participants, and consult evaluation studies and critical commentary on the different ways in which the issue has been approached. They would be able to check to see if new studies were underway that were expected to significantly update existing findings in the near future. And where answers seem to be missing or where apparent contradictions do not seem to be addressed, people would be able to propose further work to be done. They would also be able to volunteer the encrypted data associated with their own lives to support ongoing and new research.

Trying to get greater value from the public investment in social science research by increasing people's access is not going to be as simple as buying stock from Schwab. But it is interesting to note how information in both cases is about understanding and managing risk by looking at different types of information, just as in both cases that information was already being accumulated and had been for some time, if only for the exclusive use of professionals. I realize that some may find my use of Schwab a telling and distasteful conclusion to this chapter on the social contract of the social sciences. Whose side am I on anyway? I am on the side that wants the social sciences to play a much larger part in the public sector of this emerging knowledge economy with its global information systems. There is an urgent need, I would say, to check the private sector's tendency to dominate such activities, both by taking hold of handy new information technologies and by being intent on meeting people's specific interests. Automata Data would be foolish to ignore how others are going about this information business, just as it would seek to build on existing developments within the social sciences, a number of which I turn to in the next chapter.

6

Technologies of Knowing

THE INITIAL INDICATION that the world wide web might alter the world of social science research came early in its microhistory. Circa 1993, the anthropologist David Zeitlyn, from the University of Kent, had the idea of placing a digitized recording of the Mambila language on the web to accompany his article in the journal *Man*. What better way to deliver the sound of this endangered language, native to the Nigeria-Cameroon borderland, to the desktops of other anthropologists around the world? It meant that researchers could *hear* what was otherwise only transcribed in the professional literature. Scholars could now get that much closer to the spoken qualities of the language Zeitlyn was examining.

This might seem a relatively minor event in the technology of knowledge, but for a linguist studying endangered African languages, opening this sound file is like suddenly hearing a piece one had only seen in sheet music, played by its composer. It certainly seemed extraordinary to me that, four years after the file had been posted, I could listen to someone among a crowd of voices say in Mambila, "For us it's all the same who speaks." The digital recording was only ten seconds long, but after a few listenings, I could sort out the voices, follow the transcript, and almost feel the size of the room in which the recording was made. What might have seemed mildly interesting over headphones in a museum seemed uncanny coming out of the computer on my kitchen table.

While it is still too early to judge whether Zeitlyn has, in effect, launched a universal database for recording the raw data of social science research, I could not help feeling something was afoot. In some ways, things are still the same. Putting data online does little to change the sense in which researcher and reader are *listening in* on the lives of the Mambila, turning their voices into the artifacts of an endangered African language. Yet what the technology does do in this case is enable scholars to present and share the data globally, opening up the research process to more collaboration and coordination. It also opens that much more of the process to the public.

Zeitlyn is obviously a pioneer when it comes to using the web to support scholarly endeavors, and since that initial experiment he has gone on to establish the Virtual Institute of Mambila Studies on the web. Not only can one hear recordings of the language on this site, but one can play the Mambila Riddle Machine as a way of learning more about the culture of these people.[1] All of this amounts to something quite different from what has traditionally come of anthropological research. Although Zeitlyn offered what I am sure was only a sample of the recordings he made in his field studies, the web has the potential of providing access to the complete data archives for others to examine and analyze. Through the web, researchers can now offer their colleagues what was once restricted by limitations of space in print.

The publishing of research data on the web has become a habit with at least two electronic journals. The *Journal of Statistics Education* includes the data associated with its articles for the use of instructors and their students, while the *Journal of Fluids Engineering* includes the author's data set to allow for the verification and extension of the work presented. The web offers readers an opportunity to stand before the whole of the data, as the researcher stood before it. This mounting of data on the web also holds the potential of combining, extending, and comparing the information gathered among studies. Access to complete data sets would offer a check, although hardly a foolproof one, on research fraud.[2]

In the realm of scholarly book publishing, my colleague and friend Ricki Goldman-Segall has integrated a supporting web site of research data into her recent book, *Points of Viewing Children's Thinking: A Digital Ethnographer's Journey.*[3] The web site allows you to view video clips of young students talking about science as they sit in a rain forest on the Pacific coast. But we are made more than data spectators with Ricki's web site. To foster a process of collaborative analysis among those reading and viewing her work, Ricki has developed a software program known as *Web-Constellations* that allows readers to annotate and thematically analyze the video in relation to the readings arrived at by Ricki and others. In one sense, supporting a community of correspondents is all Henry Oldenburg set out to do in 1665 when he deployed the technology of print to launch the first academic periodical, the *Philosophical Transactions* of the Royal Society. The web only extends the opportunity to share one's findings and test one's hypotheses, whether the researchers deal in numbers and calculations or images and narratives.

In a similar vein, Edward Ayers, a history professor at the University of Virginia, has created the *Valley of the Shadow* web site to complement his book on the fate of two communities in the Civil War.[4] Funded by IBM and the National Endowment for the Humanities, the web site features archival materials including records on the soldiers from the two counties, maps, demographic statistics, and even the insurance claims that followed the Confederate torching of one of the bigger towns. As Ayers puts it, "not only do I have more control over the information, because it's digitized, but it will be useful long after the book is finished." He turned to the web for its inclusiveness: "We don't know what the story is, so we put all the stories there. The idea, of course, is to democratize history." Ayers also uses this Civil War web site in his teaching by asking students to test their ideas about the war against the archive, while gathering new materials to build their own public online historical resources. One student notes that "we were, like, building a book," while another held that "in this class, we had to think about how to *do* history." James McPherson, a Princeton historian whose work Ayers challenges, sees the increased access offered by the web site "a boon to the profession," even as he worries about the "coerciveness" of this much data on just two counties. But of course, those two counties don't have to be the end of it.[5]

This prospect of contributing to a public archive could well lead to researchers building data sets on a global scale that covered an increasing range of periods, populations, and circumstances. This would encourage the use of common sources and measures as well as local variations, while challenging what has been gathered with a sense of what more may be needed. These linked data sets could then be used to extend or corroborate a hypothesis, to conduct periodic reanalysis or meta-analysis, and to synthesize different orders of data, from statistical to narrative. This spirit of technologically enabled collaboration could reduce research costs, while multiplying the power of the analysis. It could support the assembling of a more coherent story among the various approaches within the social sciences.

The potential of sharing data among researchers in the social sciences was first introduced in the 1950s. Richard Rockwell, who directs the Inter-University Consortium for Political and Social Research at the University of Michigan, has described how in those early days of feeding social science data into mainframe computers, a remarkable spirit or "ethic" of cooperation, as Rockwell names it, emerged. This commitment to data sharing took hold in the social sciences well before it was taken up in the natural sciences.[6] Rockwell's organization, the Inter-University Consortium for Political and Social Research, is dedicated to facilitating access to large and important data sets. In recognition of the widespread value of some of these data sets, the National Science Foundation has designated them "national resources," much like Yellowstone Park.

In yet another variation on this theme of data-sharing, the U.S. Census produces a Public Use Micro Sample that can be used by anyone interested in exploring what the census has to offer. In addition, a number of private organizations, including some of the major polling firms, make their data available to other institutions. For his part, Rockwell offers the example of the General Social Survey (GSS), which covers some 30,000 American adults across 2,000 variables, currently extending over the period from 1972 to 1994.[7] This "national resource" is already the source of some 150 project reports and is accompanied by a running bibliography of 3,000 related studies. The GSS is the focus of ongoing roundtable discussions and electronic conferences for discussing the development of this resource. This twin concern with improving the data and the studies of it could well serve as a model for the research design side of Automata Data. The Corporation could also take a lesson from Rockwell's proposal that the GSS be used by high school students to explore how it can contribute to their understanding of the world. This would require suggestions and prepared exercises for teachers and perhaps an area set aside for high school students to compare and connect their findings, as well as conduct their own surveys, set up like a virtual (social) science fair. Automata Data could coordinate the addition to the large-scale data sets like the GSS a far broader range of data, including narratives, interviews, and videos, reflecting the full range of the social sciences' quest for knowledge. Rockwell concludes with a series of recommendations for the future of data that are consistent with the intent of Automata Data: they include promoting international studies, driven by a spirit of cooperation, rather than the typical nation-by-nation comparison. He fearlessly asks, in the important area of health services, why we don't do more with "the unexploited data resources . . . of insurance and Medicare programs."

This final point raises the technological specter of privacy loss and increased surveillance. Strangely enough, the Internet is turning out to afford a much greater degree of privacy for one's transactions—through encryption, digital cash, and anonymous rerouting—than has been possible before. In fact, law enforcement and tax agencies are increasingly concerned with virtual reality's capacity to shelter people from scrutiny.[8] All told, it would not be difficult to guarantee the legal and technical protection of personal data drawn from commercial and government databases for ongoing use in research projects. But, of course, participants—or data-donors—would only agree to this use of their data if they were convinced that the knowledge gained from the data would generate a far better understanding of important social practices and policies. The goal would be to bring the public in on this coordinated effort to determine what is needed to increase what is known. Does it all sound too unlikely?

One thing is clear—this knowledge economy is putting increasing emphasis on finding the financial advantage, if not the public value, in all forms of data. Accompanying that development is the emergence of international standards for handling data, standards that will also improve efforts at coordinating research on a global basis. The precedent for these international standards goes back to 1865, when the International Telegraph Union first took steps to ensure the prospects of a global communication system.[9] Today, the National Information Standards Organization, in Bethesda, Maryland, has already developed protocols for data transfers between computers.[10] University libraries, as well as online database and library automation vendors, are currently engaged in forming a universal database for bibliographic information.[11] You may think imagining a future of universal access among global sources of data simply wishful (or dreadful) thinking, when it can often be so difficult connecting with the computer in the next office. On the other hand, it seems to me irresponsible not to consider how the social sciences might direct these information technologies toward a wider range of human interests than those currently under development in the rapidly expanding areas of global financial services and corporate management.

Jean-Claude Guédon provides interesting historical insight into how scholars once took advantage of a shared and complete data set. He points out how closely such practices approximate the early scholarly treatment of the biblical text across Medieval Europe. There were manuscript copies of the Bible that were framed in various commentaries, each offering a different reading of the sacred text along with earlier commentaries. Those proto-hyper-linked biblical pages recreated the noisy *disputatio* of scholarly discussion. New networking technologies do much the same, in Guédon's estimation, putting "us in touch with the textual wisdom of Middle Ages and remind[ing] us that no reading can ever be totally solitary, as silent reading induced by print would lead us to believe."[12] The secret of scholarly engagement here, which Guédon does not note, was the shared text or data set that formed the core of the commentaries. Today this universal text amounts to a networking of existing and new data sources under some coordinating body or through some other form of cooperation among researchers.

These steps toward a virtually universal database could build a greater sense of global community among social scientists, even as they are directed at generating helpful sources of understanding for public and practitioners on a similar scale. While I harbor few illusions about the profound challenges of building such a universal database, objections to the very idea of such a project leave me wondering why it is preferable to wait for the continuing unmediated growth in research to provoke a collapse of public support for want of a corresponding increase in its apparent value. But I am not asking that we leap into this. To pursue Rockwell's initiative, by exploring new ways of increasing the coordinated management of research data on the web, whether through an Automata Data or not, is but to test the prospects and promise of a universal research database.

Autocitation

While the possibilities of great coordination and sharing of data are beginning to be explored, the web is increasingly being used to support the other foundation of scholarship, the citation. Links are what the web does best, after all. And the footnote was the original hyperlink, with authors suspending their work within a culture of scholarship by tying threads from it to earlier works. With the help of a good library, the reader could virtually pull up the whole of the fabric out of which the work at hand was fashioned. Today, the hotlinked world of the web, in a strange ontological reversal, makes the citational links between papers all the more real, live, and active. In much the same spirit that guided the posting of data on the web, the invitation here is to share and compare, extending the scholarly grace that comes of wanting to make the whole of one's academic enterprise part of a greater exchange of ideas. Sometimes the technology seems to simply extend the dreams, although not without massaging them.

There are proposals already afoot for establishing a *universal citation database* that would, link by link, knit together the whole of scholarly activity within a given area. In the electronic journal *First Monday*, Robert Cameron, a computer scientist at Simon Fraser University, describes, as more and more texts are posted in electronic form, how readily their references could be hyperlinked, creating a great chain of citation that would represent at least one sense of what we mean by a body of knowledge. The author of a research article would include links to the works she cited; those works in turn would be filled with links to yet other articles. What Cameron proposes is nothing less than a linking of "every scholarly work ever written—no matter how published—to every work that it cites and every work that cites it."[13] Cameron argues for this universal citation database on the most pragmatic of grounds. It is superior to the traditional journal in both serving up knowledge as a connected body of work and, given the tracking that can be done regarding who cites whom, in adjudicating academic careers. While Cameron's Universal Citation Database offers a potential saving in journal subscription costs, the whole automated citation process could simply lead to citation-bloated papers, which is only to multiply a current scholarly vice.

I want to posit an additional reason for pursuing what the web can add to this rooting of one scholarly work to another. I first realized that something was amiss when I found myself clipping citations from another researcher's online paper to paste into my own electronic bibliography. The whole process took a matter of moments, from realizing that others must have written about the practice I was referring to in my writing, to using a search engine to locate a bibliography in which references to such practices were listed, ready to be clipped and pasted. This was just a little too convenient. The technology is not the cause of such sins, but only their conveyance, making it feel more like sloth than scholarship. The powers of the web to search and link texts should give us pause over the value of this ancient scholarly task. It is all too easy to imagine a *know-bot*, a semi-intelligent software agent designed for scholars and readers that would roam the web at our beck and call, seeking out relevant citations for a phrase we've highlighted, such as "(Leonard, 1997)."[14]

Since at that point the informational value of references of that sort, that are made in passing, would be close to zero, my hope is that it might encourage greater concentration on the critical work of positioning each new piece of research and scholarship in a body of work with the care required to increase the comprehensibility of that field for a wider public. The focus would shift to what the machines cannot do. Scholars would concentrate on the core works they are responding to, challenging, and building upon, so that each new article would be judged on how its referencing of other works contributes to the overall coherence within a body of research and its discontents. Outside of this careful positioning among a limited number of key works, the piling up of passing references could be left to the machines. Which is only to say that the technology may expose what has too often become the emptiness of the bibliographic gesture—now that autociting is available to reader and writer alike—and lead scholars back to the original purpose of the referencing of other works. The careful use of citations can reveal the evolution and scope of thinking on a topic, creating a sense of broad and whole cloth, changing in its texture and feel. Or citations can suggest a patchwork of fragments loosely stitched together, with barely a shared thread running among them. The technology is once again a provocation for thinking about why we do what we do, when machines do it better.

While I believe we urgently need to explore new ways of organizing and presenting knowledge, I realize that changing the technology does not necessarily change habits of mind or hand. The best example of that stubbornness sits at my fingertips, in the form of the QWERTY keyboard that puts the letter *e* in a less than convenient spot, given its frequency of use in English. This keyboard arrangement was, after all, designed to keep mechanical typewriter keys from jamming by effectively slowing typists down. New technologies tend to accommodate old habits even as they afford new opportunities for change. My hope, obviously, is that the social sciences will want to test the powers of these new technologies in the years ahead, rather than just use them for business as usual, only easier and faster. Yet if any technology poses a sweeping threat to the habits of our trade, it is data mining, which mechanizes social science research as its developers brazenly go about automating what they call "Knowledge Discovery in Databases."

Data Mining and Knowledge Discovery

Data mining is the name of a recent generation of software devoted to "discovering" complex forms of information within databases. It combines techniques from machine learning, pattern recognition, and statistics "to automatically extract concepts, concept interrelations and patterns of interest from large databases," as a tutorial sponsored by the Association for the Advancement of Artificial Intelligence puts it.[15] The editor of the new journal *Datamining and Knowledge Discovery in Databases*, Usama M. Fayyad, from the research division of Microsoft, sets the tone for this field by conjuring up the "menacing profiles of ever-growing mountains of data." Yet the real concern here is not with information overload, but with the lost value of data, especially large data sets, that might otherwise be mined for new knowledge.

Data mining is a software routine ready to ride through the data-glut on a white horse, salvaging informational value wherever it roams: "Be it a satellite orbiting our planet, a medical imaging device, a credit-card transaction verification system, or a supermarket's checkout system," Fayyad writes, "the human at the other end of the data gathering and storage machinery is faced with the same problem: What to do with all this data? Ignoring whatever we cannot analyze would be wasteful and unwise." As he sees it, scientists, manufacturers, and retailers can gain competitive advantage by turning data into knowledge.

Knowledge discovery in databases comes about through a series of steps, which Fayyad lays out in the special language of this emergent discipline. First of all, the data needs to be properly *warehoused* in a usable form. This means that the critical factors for analysis need to be *targeted*, after which the selected data is *cleaned* of obvious errors and *preprocessed* in ways that *transform* and *reduce* it into more manageable forms. Now that the data is prepared, the actual *data mining* software program goes to work, applying algorithms designed to detect and identify apparent patterns and anomalies. Once determined, these patterns and anomalies are used to generate *models* that specify what knowledge can be said to lie within the data. After arriving at a suitably powerful model, the user can extract knowledge, which can then be *consolidated* and *used*. You may be tempted to ask which steps in this elaborate process are completed by humans, and which by machines. But that would be the wrong question. It suggests that a fruitful distinction can be made between humans and machines in the extraction and refinement of knowledge, whereas data mining is about the technological extension of human sense-making and value-seeking capacities.

Fayyad offers a hypothetical example of a bank seeking to identify which accounts have entries that possess a 75 percent or better chance of being fraudulent. This is not your standard database query, which would be more along the lines of identifying bank customers depositing over $1,000 per month. The data mining approach, Fayyad explains, is to begin with a set of known fraudulent and nonfraudulent entries, and use them to develop an algorithm for the data mining software that is capable of isolating the questionable entries. "This is an example," Fayyad explains, "of a much needed and much more natural interface between humans and databases." Knowledge discovery in databases (KDD) partakes of "the 'art' of statistical analysis." It makes analysis "easier to use by those who own the data, regardless of whether they have the pre-requisite knowledge of the techniques being used." Data mining is, ultimately, "a science of how to exploit massive data sets." Fayyad is moving here among claims of art, science, and convenience. This is what can happen with the commodification and distribution of expertise that distinguishes this knowledge economy (for more on the political implications of this, see the next chapter).

Recycling data-waste into knowledge profit does pose a danger Fayyad is prepared to acknowledge: "Blind mining . . . can easily deteriorate into *data dredging*." The charge of dredging has a familiar ring for me, as I recall some years ago giving in to the temptation of repeatedly running different analyses of my dissertation data in search of the statistically significant correlations that indicated I had found something, or so I thought. As Bob Rogers, a professor of psychology at Dalhousie University who ended his helpful explanations with "and Bob's your uncle," pointed out to me, unless you start with a probable hypothesis or model, this fishing for significant correlations only increases the risk that what you have found is a statistical coincidence.

Nonetheless, over the last few decades a rather contrary school of "exploratory data analysis" has developed, much to the appreciation of those working in KDD. One proposes a model in KDD only after examining the patterns and anomalies garnered by earlier rounds of data mining. Rather than collecting data to test the strength of a given proposition, as in the traditional research model, data mining begins with a sea of existing data on the assumption that it holds untold knowledge waiting to be extracted.[16] While applications for data mining are developing in sports, helping teams capitalize on the considerable statistical accumulations that take place during a game, and even in music, enabling computers to utilize the signature patterns of the great composers to write their own music, our interest lies in what this technology can offer the social sciences.[17]

In the field of health care and epidemiology, the Northern Ireland Knowledge Engineering Laboratory is mining lifestyle and genetic data in search of the causes of psoriasis by comparing the patterns found within this data to factors affecting related skin diseases. The Lab is also exploring what can be learned from mining the considerable statistics available on cancer patients, as well as from comparing the patterns of diabetic care.[18] A number of the major issues I have introduced in this book, from breast cancer to bilingual education, have given rise to great quantities of data that could also be explored by this process. Data mining will not produce answers to the questions that most trouble us, but this ability to sweep through, as well as monitor on an ongoing basis, the vast quantities of information being otherwise assembled needs to be tested for its value in alerting, suggesting, and provoking social scientists.

Although data mining is in many ways still an emerging technology, it already represents a $40 million industry, according to Forester Research, and is predicted to exceed $800 million by the turn of the century. The next step for this meeting of science and industry appears to be *information* mining, which will sift through and sort enormous quantities of running text (reports and correspondence, as opposed to numerical and coded data) in search of the answers needed to support corporate decision making. The Age of Information has escalated the portion of the economy devoted to trafficking in it. Information not only supports and informs economic processes, as it once did; information is what is for sale. A more effective endeavor than simply holding such developments in intellectual contempt would be to look for ways of extending the reach of an alternative information economy devoted to public good. As a *New Yorker* cartoon, featuring the proverbial newscaster, recently had it, "And, in a move sure to attract the attention of regulators, the private sector made a bid to acquire the public sector."

Having looked at the high end of the information technologies, from know-bots to data mining, I close this chapter by examining a more modest use of machinery devoted to providing research findings to practicing physicians. After considering imagined and prototypical technologies, I want to return to earth with an existing program that carries with it much of the spirit of what I envision for an Automata Data. As I have suggested with breast cancer, research on health care often relies on basic social science technologies of knowledge, and with Evidence-Based Medicine, the focus is on improving the flow of this type of research into the hands of the practitioner.

Evidence-Based Medicine

The Centre for Evidence-Based Medicine at Radcliffe Hospital in Oxford is directed by Professor David L. Sackett, who has worked for thirty years to help doctors make use of medical research in their daily practice. Sackett's web page offers a picture of a white-bearded eminence in a duffel coat squinting at the camera, hair caught in the wind. He stands atop a tank that appears to be on active duty. Once you have learned something of the determination he brings to his work, you might well come to imagine that the picture represents his Tiananmen Square stand against the conventional wisdom that governs daily medical practice.

That wisdom, it turns out, is typically acquired by doctors early in their careers, as they remain only marginally aware of the churning of the research mills. One study reveals that a large sample of doctors, facing the same "garden variety urinary tract infection," recommended no less than 180 different treatments, suggesting that where they were trained as well as when must play a part. Another study pointed to what amounts to a thirteen-year delay between the research-proven effectiveness of a treatment and its systematic use in medical practice.[19]

Sackett and his colleagues believe that the practice of evidence-based medicine (EBM) will help physicians take advantage of what the latest medical research has to offer, and they define evidence-based medicine as "the conscientious, explicit and judicious use of current best evidence in making decisions about the care of individual patients."[20] It seems an obvious enough principle, yet to put it into practice they have had to construct a bridge from the laboratory life of research journals to the waiting room full of patients. Thanks to their considerable efforts, a physician can turn now from the patient sitting on the examining table to a computer holding the Best Evidence CD-ROM with its review of the research on relevant conditions, symptoms, treatments, and diagnostic tests. The physician may have suspicions confirmed by the clinical findings on the CD-ROM; she may be reassured or challenged by the probabilities presented. She may see a pattern with other patients or feel encouraged to try a new course of treatment. She may want to raise her case with others at the Centre for Evidence-Based Medicine. And the patient may well appreciate learning more about the research on the diagnosis and treatment of the condition.[21] Let us go a little further into how this system works.

The *EBM Journal*, edited by Sackett and Brian Haynes at McMaster University, presents journal abstracts culled from roughly 70 journals that have been screened by "a panel of front-line clinicians," as the journal describes it. Panel members chose research that is "both valid and of current clinical importance." Surprisingly enough, this focus on research that deals with patient care eliminates 98 percent of the medical literature reviewed. The *EBM Journal* ends up presenting "busy clinicians with an easily digestible summary (average reading time is about 30 minutes) every 8 weeks."[22] This very high rejection level suggests one of two things—that it takes 98 parts "pure research" to produce two parts applicable knowledge; or, as appears to be the case, researchers demonstrate little interest in clinical research.[23] One question posed by the entire EBM project—and this would certainly of relevance to an Automata Data—is whether setting up this pipeline from research to physician will draw greater attention to the potential effectiveness of clinical research, and thus result in a greater proportion of articles of "clinical importance." For Sackett and his colleagues in EBM, the randomized clinical trial is the "gold standard," simply because it is "so much more likely to inform us and so much less likely to mislead us" when it comes to prescribing treatments.[24] Despite its minor place within the medical literature, Sackett estimates that a million randomized trials using social science research methods have been completed over the last thirty years.[25] EBM also uses meta-analysis of multiple studies, cross-sectional studies of patient records, and follow-up studies on earlier trials, as well as some of the basic or pure research in areas such as genetics and immunology. The current charge for an annual subscription to the *EBM Journal*, for example, is roughly $100 for the journal or CD-ROM. It seems an eminently reasonable price for research to serve practice so directly.

The *EBM Journal* editorial team also works on the American College of Physicians' *Journal Club*, which offers doctors a selection of patient-focused research on internal medicine from twenty-five core journals.[26] The standards for the selection of research are strict: for example, "the economic question addressed must be based on comparison of alternatives," and "alternative diagnostic or therapeutic services or quality improvement activities must be compared on the basis of both the outcomes produced (effectiveness) and resources consumed (costs)." The journals present abstracts in a standard format, accompanied by a commentary by a clinician.[27] The commentary offers compelling and blunt advice directed at treatment of, for example, stroke victims: "One patient in 11 will be prevented from dying or needing long-term institutional care if treated in an organized Stroke Unit rather than a General Medicine Ward." This particular commentary concluded with an unequivocal prescription for clinical practice: "Because the implementation costs are relatively small, every hospital should now organize its stroke service according to these principles."[28]

Another feature of EBM is its use of probabilities to define the current state of knowledge about a disease or treatment. Consider the stark reading of a medication's effectiveness provided by what is called the Number Needed to Treat (NNT) calculation:

"The Number Needed to Treat (NNT) is the number of patients you need to treat to prevent one additional bad outcome (death, stroke, etc.). For example, if a drug has an NNT of 5, it means you have to treat 5 people with the drug to prevent one additional bad outcome." This may not be the most accurate representation of probability as a form of knowledge, but you can clearly see how they are trying to render the concept readily comprehensible, which is, of course, the challenge facing the public knowledge project that is Automata Data. The EBM program offers a range of incisive measures, providing participating physicians with detailed instructions on how they are calculated. It also invites physicians to comment on and contribute to the knowledge it presents.

However, the Centre for Evidence-Based Medicine is aware of how hard it is to change anyone's practice. It has wisely chosen to prepare instructional materials that support its introduction into continuing medical education programs. It investigates the research most needed by clinicians, while supporting the expansion of patient-based research, with a focus on clinical trials that are just now beginning to see increased support among funding agencies. As I write, the United States Congress and the president are both supporting substantial increases in biomedical research funding, including a fivefold increase in the number of participants in clinical trials in oncology. One of the key architects of this proposal, Richard D. Klausner, director of the National Cancer Institute, notes that while 300,000 people are currently participating in these trials, the goal is "to insure that all people who wish to participate in a clinical trial are able to do so." We are in the midst, he proudly claims, of "a golden age of discovery."[29] This idea of elevating participation in research to a human right, while clearly far more of an ethical issue in medicine than in other areas, bears noting in light of what I am proposing with Automata Data.

The United States already supports a network of seventy-five General Clinical Research Centers that provide a full range of support for researchers doing clinical research under National Institute of Health and other federal grants. These centers operate under the auspices of the National Center for Research Resources (NCRR), which offers its own model of what a unit devoted to supporting and coordinating research can do in the biomedical field. The NCRR "creates, develops, and provides a comprehensive range of human, animal, technological, and other resources to enable biomedical research advances."[30]

Although clinical trials are clearly an important source of evidence for EBM, "outcome analysis" (also known as "population-based research") is a useful source of knowledge for medical practitioners.[31] Outcome analysis represents the data mining of medical research. It works with the large medical history databases possessed by hospitals and insurance companies, which hold patient records for tests, treatments, and results. This method has the distinct advantage of including patients who are otherwise excluded from randomized trials because their health is too precarious. This use of existing records can also reduce the expense of the research while expanding the size and range of the sample. Since the early 1990s, for example, the state of New York has published the mortality figures for bypasss surgery in the state. In another instance of outcome analysis, an international study of the records for 230,000 elderly heart-attack victims was able to determine that Americans in this sample were eight times more likely than Canadians to undergo related surgery, such as angioplasty and bypass, while the survival rates after the first year were much the same. The value of these studies, whether to the EBM program or the insurance companies, indicates that the quality and comprehensiveness of this information is only going to increase.[32]

The *New York Times* has recently referred to EBM as an "intellectual golden spike," presumably for how well it completes the link across the great divide between medical research and practice. However, EBM is not without its critics, including rather skeptical physician-academics who wonder how "probabilistic thinking" can be relevant to the treatment of a single patient.[33] A somewhat impatient Dr. Sackett is all too ready to throw the alternative back in their faces, with the sharp retort, "Art kills." He also refers to leeches, rather aggressively suggesting that some traditions die hard but wisely. My own conciliatory inclinations lead me to answer, yes, database searches are not enough in treating individual patients and never will be. But EBM is not intended to do it all. It merely seeks to inform, to make the known available, on which the doctor must still act. What EBM also does, though, is address the otherwise invisible specter of *knowledge waste* that keeps what is known from serving those it might help. And as for the fear of probabilities, I can only wonder when a doctor is *not* playing the odds, hedging bets, and building in margins of safety, whether in making a diagnosis or prescribing a treatment.

Perhaps the most serious objection raised to EBM comes from Ivan Illich's critique of what he terms the "disabling professions." Illich holds that professions such as medicine are taking undue control of our lives, with technology only assisting in extending the force of a collective expertise that leaves us essentially disabled: "It is no longer the individual professional who imputes a 'need' to the individual client, but a corporate agency that imputes to entire classes of people their needs, and claims the mandate to test the whole population in order to identify all those who belong to the group of potential patients."[34] On the other hand, Illich describes what he calls tools of conviviality as "those which give each person who uses them the greatest opportunity to enrich the environment with the fruits of his or her vision."[35] Would that Automata Data could one day make such a claim.

Corporate interventions into our lives do pose a serious risk to individual autonomy and democratic processes (a topic I address in relation to Automata Data in the next chapter). Although I believe that EBM, no less than Automata Data, is about informing rather than diminishing individual autonomy, such assumptions need to be constantly tested and tempered, just as the corporate structures will need to be constantly modified, without ruling out the possibility that they will have to be abandoned. Such experiments with knowledge have been known to fail, after all.

Another point of caution here is that this is not the first time medicine has been at the forefront of technological innovation. The first "expert systems," which claimed artificial intelligence for computer circuitry, were directed at creating super-doctors, combining the advantages of perfect knowledge with infallible logic. Where are those earlier machines now? Perhaps the best known is MYCIN, which was developed in 1972 at Stanford University. It was designed to assist in the diagnosis of blood diseases, especially where diagnostic time can be a critical factor. Although this system, which was guided by some 500 rules, proved more accurate than a sample of Stanford's medical faculty, it was not used in regular practice. "It was as much because of ethical and legal issues," Alison Cawsey explains in her online course on Databases and Artificial Intelligence at Heriot-Watt University, Edinburgh, "related to the use of computers in medicine—if it gives the wrong diagnosis, who do you sue?"[36] What sets EBM apart from earlier generations of medical information technologies is that it is not building its hopes on the powers of artificial intelligence. It draws on the same "knowledge base" as the expert systems, but its focus is on informing what is still the physician's decision-making process.

Another health knowledge system, and one that really takes advantage of the web, is OncoLink, run by the University of Pennsylvania Cancer Center.[37] Its mission is to serve as a clearinghouse for what is currently known about cancer, and it addresses physician, patient, and public, without making distinctions among them, which makes it closer to the Automata Data model than the EBM program. This online resource provides not only the results of trial and treatment programs, but updates on ongoing studies and invitations to participate in clinical trials. Here is a model of knowledge as an urgent and active public sphere of activity. OncoLink also offers survivor stories and even has a children's art gallery. It speaks to another kind of knowledge that might support one against what comes of knowing this disease.

All of this suggests that perhaps the case for evidence-based education or evidence-based criminal justice may be as compelling as the case for medicine, given the amount of "evidence" that continues to accumulate. As I discussed earlier, the legal profession is increasingly relying upon electronic database libraries that would make the strange-sounding evidence-based legal practice all that much easier to manage. Yet what I am proposing with Automata Data is somewhat more ambitious that simply an evidence-based service for practitioners, such as lawyers, teachers, or doctors. I am determined to see this knowledge serve both public and practitioner, which is more in line with Oncolink, across the much larger range of research activity represented by the social sciences.

In 1979, when he assumed his role as prophet of the postmodern, Jean-François Lyotard warned scholars about the impact of the computer on their work. He wrote that "along with the hegemony of computers comes a certain logic, and therefore a certain set of prescriptions determining which statements are accepted as 'knowledge' statements."[38] The truth of that statement, then and now, is only partial, in true postmodern spirit. It suggests that computers, of themselves, exert a control over our lives and work. We need to ask where the design of the computers came from, if not from dreams of knowing the world, of being able to calculate and take its measure, dreams that continue to guide the way we tinker with these machines, turning them to our work, finding our metaphors for knowledge and the mind extended by their devices. Mind-machine dichotomies strike me as no more helpful than mind-body dichotomies. We are one with the machines we build, whether they keep our milk cold or raise our garage doors; they are what we have made of our lives as much as a poem or a prayer is.

We need to see that we have a choice. We can ignore the developments within these technologies of knowledge. We can mount an incisive critique of their form and impact. But along with this critique, we can also engage in a program of experimentation that uses the technology to test and expand our vision of how they might serve the public sector, how they might assist the social sciences, say, in their service to policy makers, professionals in the field, and the general public. There may be no shaking the idea that an autonomous technology drives human history.[39] But here is the chance to intervene radically in the social sciences' use of information technologies, demonstrating something other than acquiescence to mechanical hegemonies. It starts with how apparent it is that the machines have not yet been built to everyone's advantage. From there, those of us within the social sciences can look for ways in which our privileged access to these technologies can be used to redress the imbalance of advantage, without necessarily turning our backs on the machines. We need to find a way of using these technologies for something more than simply speeding up academic "productivity." We need to find a way of ensuring that the knowledge we produce can do more for the human interests we associate with democracy.[40]

7

Enlightenment, Democracy, Knowledge

I T TAKES A CERTAIN CHUTZPAH to name the period you live in the Age of Enlightenment, and it takes something more than that to make it stick. The choice of the term "enlightenment" suggests that this earlier era had dreams that exceeded those of an age such as ours which is given to the rapid flow of information. Yet what Kant, Voltaire, and others claimed for their Age of Enlightenment in the eighteenth century is not lost to us, as it survived subsequent eras of Revolution, Romanticism, Imperialism, and Modernity. Today, as we continue trying to reason our way to a fair and just world, we are guided by the light of that earlier era. In fact, the human hope for enlightenment stands remarkably undiminished by the terrible and repeated failures to achieve those original dreams of justice and equality. However faltering the West's efforts, however often it has had to deal with its own failures, the very spirit of this effort owes something to what was also known as the Age of Reason.

In this sense, Automata Data is yet another engine of Enlightenment, a rattly knowledge contraption retrofitted with Age of Information technologies. Its operating system combines the features of an encyclopedia, a public library, and a public broadcasting system, delivering the body of social science research to wherever a computer can be jacked into the Internet. The intention is to extend by some modest amount the rule of reason and understanding, to provide grounds for greater justice and equality in the course of the world. This chapter is about the politics of knowledge for such public good. It hinges on Immanuel Kant's Enlightenment belief that reason and knowledge need to be in the hands of the people, and deals with the challenge this poses in opening research activity to the play of public knowledge.

Kant declared his support for the intellectual rights and autonomy of the people in an op-ed piece for the newspaper *Berlinische Monatsschrift* in 1784. He was responding to the question, put to him by the paper, "What is Enlightenment?"[1] In this brief article, he explained that while humanity had not yet achieved that final delivery from blind faith and unreason, the age was still suffused with prospects for working through reason's always critical course. With the Enlightenment about to find its culmination and eclipse in the French Revolution, Kant took the time to publicly affirm what had been the promise of his own Age.

"Enlightenment is man's release from his self-incurred tutelage," Kant declared, adding that "tutelage is man's inability to make use of his understanding without direction from another."[2] This must certainly have seemed a strange declaration for a professor of philosophy to make. How could the Enlightenment be about a release from what sounds a lot like *education*, with his references to tutelage and taking direction from another? Kant was, in effect, redefining the educational project in the name of autonomy. The Kantian goal of learning and thinking was to work oneself free from the oppressive direction of others. Enlightenment was a critical ability to think one's own way through what church, state, and school had made of the world.

It needs to be stated that Kant's vision of human autonomy was seriously compromised by the racism of the age, which he did not subject to his otherwise sweeping critiques, just as it was based on what now seems an unrealistic regard for an isolating individualism.[3] Still, our current idea of democracy owes a debt to this ideal of self-determination, which has helped focus the struggle to move beyond that ill-reasoned sensibility that divides by race and isolates the disempowered. Kant himself remains proof of how what is thought just and reasonable at any given point needs to be kept open, tentative, and constantly attended to, knowing how easily things are got wrong, how easily the scales tip to the advantage of some over others.

Social science research serves this democratic ideal, both through its own openness to critique and through its efforts to equip the critique of the given and decided. You can hear these sentiments echoed in Rogers Smith's recent call for research that redresses imbalances that "arise from discrepancies in power, wealth, and prestige among interested parties who shape opinion on the issues in question; from disproportionate control of education and communications systems by advocates of one viewpoint; from traditions and customs that constitute a familiar status quo with which many feel all too comfortable."[4] In just this way, the Enlightenment interest in freeing the public from intellectual tyranny needs to be directed at what I would cast as a democratic politics of knowledge.

An Automata Data guided by this spirit would seek to increase the social sciences' contribution to public self-determination, by exploring new ways of directing research at questions critical to the progress of those determinations. That is, it would seek to serve and lead in the deliberations, no less than any other participant in this democratic process. Automata Data would, though, have to be especially sensitive, in pushing the social sciences into greater public play, to its role as a check on the sometimes less-than-democratic tendencies of expert knowledge to dictate the right and true way forward. Far too often the pursuit of expertise has been directed, in the elitist spirit of paternalism, against people's autonomy. It was, after all, somewhat less than a century after Kant went public with the Enlightenment's liberating promise that a bitter cry was heard against this rule of reason, especially as it had taken the form of a new science of society.

In 1864, Fyodor Dostoevsky published *Notes From Underground*, a fictional diatribe against the dangers of this assuming knowledge that had already begun to smack of social engineering.[5] The sullen and ill-natured narrator of this monologue—"I am a sick man . . . . I am a spiteful man"—rails about the crystal palaces of reason within which he, for one, would not reside. This man was not, in what has become a famous image, to be played like a piano key, with the narrator taking a jab at the great instrument of bourgeois gentrification. He refused the dictates of a reason that presumed to predict and determine the shape of his life.

However much Dostoevsky's existential cry was directed at the Age of Reason, it was equally consistent with the Enlightenment stress on intellectual autonomy and critique. Dostoevsky was only demanding humankind's release from the tutelage assumed by the newfound and positivist social sciences: "You will shout at me (that is, you will still favor me with your shout) that, after all," this former and disgruntled civil servant protests, "no one is depriving me of my will, that all they are concerned with is that my will should somehow of itself, of its own free will, coincide with my own normal interests, with the laws of nature and arithmetic. Bah, gentleman, what sort of free will is left when we come to tables and arithmetic?"[6]

Dostoevsky knew only too well the abuse of law and power, having suffered in Czarist Russia not only arrest (for what was essentially associating with the wrong crowd), but also a terrifying mock execution, followed by years of exile in Siberia. It is hardly surprising that he makes the narrator of the Notes a little short on patience over promises of how this new light of a human science can be trusted to serve humankind: "Now you, for instance, want to cure men of their old habits and reform their will in accordance with science and common sense. But how do you know that, not only that it is possible, but that it is desirable, to reform man in that way? And what leads you to the conclusion that it is so necessary to reform man's desires? In short, how do you know that such a reformation will really be advantageous to man?"[7]

We are then reminded that whatever efforts are made to order humanity by "table and arithmetic," whatever progress is achieved in this determination of human behavior, contrary forces are also at work within us. "Man likes to create and build roads, that is beyond dispute," Dostoevsky's narrator allows, before hitting back with the question, "But why does he also have such a passionate love for destruction and chaos?" And this misanthrope is not without an answer, one that may speak to why

Automata Data might seem such an unlikely prospect: "He is instinctively afraid," he offers, "of attaining his goal and completing the edifice he is constructing."[8] This instinct may, more than any other factor, doom any Automata Data project. It has me playing the gentleman of arithmetic to Dostoevsky's deeper dyspeptic reading of the chaotic truth within. The continuing disarray of the social sciences could be left to stand as a tribute to our chaotic tendencies and our need to rail and roil against those who would cure us of our old habits, but I am obviously troubled by such a wasteful path to Dostoevskian salvation.

The social sciences have, in many ways, moved beyond the tyranny of Dostoevsky's "positive knowledge of human behavior," which would determine people "in accordance with science." The social sciences could do more, I contend, with Kant's Enlightenment hope of helping people "make use of [their] understanding without direction from another." As I imagine it, Automata Data would offer a countermeasure against people's increasing dependence on the tutelage and arithmetic of others, within a knowledge economy of experts, consultants, professionals, and agents (real and virtual). "Indeed in ordinary parlance," historian Thomas Haskell offers, summarizing our modern state of mind in less than ordinary parlance, "one of the best reasons we can offer for choosing a course of action is that it comports with the advice of recognized authority."[9] It may indeed seem a fine line, but Automata Data is not about adherence to this or that course under the spell of recognized authorities. Rather, it seeks to provide the public with the means to move beyond accepting or defying the *advice* of the expert, by enabling the public to consult and challenge the quality and range of knowledge behind that advice.

Within the emerging social sciences of the last century, such key figures as Karl Marx and Herbert Spencer were already worrying about the undue influence of intellectuals (other than themselves) on those whom this new endeavor was intended to serve. The fears were justified, as more than a few social scientists have since proven all too ready to promote the authority of their knowledge as authority to govern humankind.[10] At the very turn of the century, the early sociologist Edward Ross frankly titled a book of his *Social Control*, making it the explicit point of a sociology for "those who administer the moral capital of society." There was no mistaking the moral imperative that drove this science for Ross: "In this way, [the sociologist] will make himself an accomplice of all good men for the undoing of all bad men."[11] Then there was B. F. Skinner teaching pigeons to play Ping-Pong as a model of what could be done in the social engineering of humankind, or as he fearlessly put it: "A scientific analysis of behavior dispossesses autonomous man and turns the control he has been said to exert over to the environment."[12] Today, with Skinner's behaviorism largely eclipsed, cognitive scientists are building neural networks intended to operate as "relatively autonomous agents," in William Bechtel's judgment. Such networks could be directed to make decisions on our behalf, but fortunately only in the "relatively remote future," Bechtel reassures us. A professor in the philosophy-neuroscience-psychology program at Washington University, Bechtel at least insists that we will have every reason to hold these networks "morally responsible for their behavior."[13] A reassuring thought, for lawyers perhaps.

This is only to say that the refinement of expertise adds to the authority of the expert, unless a deliberate effort is made to make it otherwise.[14] It will take no small effort, then, to ensure that improvements in the social sciences are directed at "releasing" people from the direction of others, rather than adding to their dependence on such direction. It would take very little to turn this mechanical gigabeast of an Automata Data, this corporate golem of analytical force, into another form of professional self-aggrandizement, joining mandarin and technocrat in an elitism of expertise. Automata Data could easily be directed at further insulating the closed circle of expert consultation and policy formation, if it is not deliberately structured as a public resource directed at increasing, critiquing, and redressing the accountability of political processes.

When it comes to offering a check on this runaway and co-opted professionalism, there is always, after Dostoevsky, the critical edge offered by Ivan Illich. Illich predicted some years ago—although "optimistically advocated" is a better term for it—an end to the "age of professional dominance."[15] He imagined this dominance overtaken by the growth of personal autonomy and democratic rights. In an equally idealistic mood, I am posing Automata Data as a challenge to the social sciences, although it may seem unrealistic to suggest this field exercises anything approaching "professional dominance" over society.

Still, I want to ask whether the social sciences can turn their less-than-dominant professionalism into a more powerful public resource for expanding the democratic sphere of our daily activity. Can the knowledge it affords strengthen personal autonomy and public discourse, rather than advance this disabling professional dominance? I am not thinking about turning back the clock on this knowledge game to a time before the professions and their institutions were such major players. But as we go forward I obviously feel we still have it within our power to renew the social contract the social sciences have undertaken to support an understanding of the world, as I read it, that advances the democratic project.

Up to this point it has seemed that our best protection against the social sciences falling into clutches of the powerful has been to ensure that it remains in such a thorough muddle that it is virtually incapacitated as a political force. Even this "strategy" has not proved foolproof. A little research can be a dangerous thing in the hands of the powerful, especially when it takes significant resources to challenge the studies so wielded. To put it another way, the current muddle fails to serve the powerful and the general public equally. Surely the time has come for an ethics of knowledge that holds equality of access foremost among its principles, encompassing a right to the full range of available information and a right to participate in setting the agenda for the pursuit of that information. What better purpose could there be for an information technology that prides itself on building a global network?

This epistemic ethics has me siding with Gertrude Himmelfarb, the notably conservative historian, who has recently proposed, tongue only partially in cheek, that Bill Gates is an agent of Jacques Derrida, "the high priest of postmodernism." But that is not the part we agree on. Rather, we concur that this new postmodern operating system stands to open many windows on knowledge a little farther than before: "The democratization of knowledge is all to the good," she observes, "if it means the democratization of *access* to knowledge."[16]

What directs my project, then, is simply the question of whether the social sciences can begin to do more to diminish the intervention of one mind upon another. This would define the work of Automata Data. Put another way, imagine that in order to sustain its incorporation, Automata Data would have to face a Kantian Enlightenment Test, which I envision as consisting of three questions:

1. Does Automata Data foster a broader understanding of social science research among more people than current practices have provided?

2. Does this greater understanding advance the critical and constructive role this research plays in democratic processes and individual choices?

3. Is Automata Data open and responsive to criticism of its operations, especially in light of the first two questions?[17]

Obviously, the responses to such questions will remain open to constant debate. Such is the persistent and welcomed legacy of that earlier critical age.

Even if these criteria are met by the storefront social science of Automata Data, it will not prevent some people from tapping into this new source of knowledge to further their own intellectual guardianship over people. Others, perhaps many others, will continue to welcome this tutelage, which will seem all the more informed and authoritative with Automata Data to back it up. Yet Automata Data's mandate will be continually to seek new ways of addressing public and practitioners directly, great defender that it is of the Enlightenment. It will challenge people to see for themselves, to make up their own minds, in light of the range of knowledge spawned by different forms of research and the discussion over how this knowledge is related and distinguished within the social sciences. Does it seem all too much for public consumption? Well, I do think that it should be a mutually educational project for both public and profession. And as I've already suggested, it is hardly more than is currently being offered to those with an interest in professional sports and investment finance.

For the general public to be in a position to judge the exercise of power through all of its institutional manifestations, whether beneficial or arbitrary, has long been recognized as a critical form of knowledge for democracy. Alexis de Tocqueville noted its importance among American citizens in the early years of the emerging nation: "Equality begets in man the desire of judging of everything for himself, it gives him in all things a taste for the tangible and the real." He goes on to note a democratic impatience with obfuscation:

> It is on their own testimony [that democratic citizens] are accustomed to rely. They like to discern the object which engages their attention with extreme clearness [and] they therefore strip off as much as possible all that covers it. This disposition of mind soon leads them to condemn forms which they regard as useless or [as] inconvenient veils placed between them and the truth.[18]

Yaron Ezrahi, a political scientist at the Hebrew University in Jerusalem, takes this theme of democratic witnessing a step further by noting how the modern liberal state has "appropriated and adapted technology as a political resource for the construction of its particular system of accountability."[19] What I envision for an Automata Data is a technological means of increasing the social sciences' contribution to what Ezrahi calls the "civil epistemology" of the modern liberal state. He rightly worries that technology will be used by the state to escape "politically damaging exposures and attributions of responsibility," if we do not take deliberate steps to utilize it as a way of extending the citizen's gaze and engagement.[20]

Among the democratic supports for this politically engaging knowledge that Automata Data would provide is a way of tracing the facts back to the projects that produced them, rather than having them appear as absolute and established. It will treat knowledge within "webbed accounts" of understanding rather than as a "master theory," to follow the phrasing of Donna Haraway, a sociologist of science at the University of California at Santa Cruz. For Haraway, these webbed accounts amount to "a map of tensions and resonances," which could well form a guiding image for Automata Data's representation of the diversity of research approaches and findings.[21] (The trap one has to watch for here is that the map itself may become the master theory.)

In assembling the range of research within the social sciences, Automata Data would consolidate some studies, while juxtaposing others, some represented in coordinated sets of numbers, others in disparate digitized images. It would offer access to the local and discontinuous knowledges of the systems by which we live, as well as links among those systems set with the social sciences' ongoing efforts to establish various systems of sense and meaning, giving numbers and narratives to those deeply affected lives. I would suggest that Automata Data would be well advised to do this in a manner that dispels the pretense that what the social sciences have to offer, if only they'd get their act together, is the single and underlying truth of this social reality. Instead, one is able to follow how that reality is variously inscribed by the social sciences' different methods and stances, extending rather than resolving the public debate and development over social issues. This diversity of approaches is not, then, a sign of the immaturity of the social sciences, as has often been contended.[22] The state of knowledge within the social sciences offers no less than is found through other forms of human expression—namely, a profusion of ways of knowing. This diversity, remember, calls for webbed accounts and maps of tensions and resonances; these accounts and maps are always open to challenge over how they represent this field of research, of course, but not simply on the grounds that they fail to achieve the underlying unity of knowledge.

Allowing for this diversity of knowing may make my naïveté all the more striking, as I imagine that placing this diverse body of knowledge in public hands, even if it can be made readily comprehensible, will contribute to the conduct of democratic processes. And I can only respond by suggesting that if the profession makes no greater effort to render this knowledge a more intelligible and accessible public resource, it will begin to smell a little like bad faith. There may be reasons I am conveniently overlooking why this is a bad idea for both public and profession. And certainly Automata Data may not be the best way to go about it. But to dismiss the general project out of hand because of an untested assumption, that people would not be interested in, capable of using, or helped by the project, seems to me to represent a patronizing stand against enlightenment.

I say an untested assumption, because I am still allowing that this knowledge could prove of limited value and interest. What if, after a flurry of initial interest, Automata Data fails as a public utility? This diffuse and accessible realm of knowledge could well turn out to be of no greater value to public or practitioner than it is in its current state. People may feel it is simply not worth navigating their way through this careful and ever-dynamic assembly of social science knowledge and what it might offer to the democratic contest of ideas and inclinations, programs and policies. What if we build it and they do not come—or worse, do not fund? Worse still, what if people's interest in participating in social science research declines after Automata Data demonstrates once and for all the true value of social science research?

It could happen, and that is why Automata Data is such an important test—first as a thought experiment, through which the social sciences contemplate why going public is or is not important at this time; and then as a pilot study, perhaps, in a given area such as bilingual education to gauge public interest and response. If it were to become clear, through the running of an Automata Data, that social science research lacks this general public value, then I believe that researchers would need to change the way they think about their work. If it turned out that the public and practitioners alike found little direct or immediate value in this increased access to the riches of the social sciences, then I am sure many of us would want to start over again, rethinking the function and relevance of this inquiry into the dynamics of social life. Yet I say this knowing all the while that there are instances in which social science research has been able to draw more than its share of public attention, if in deeply troubling ways.[23]

The Bell Curve and Automata Data

If I had to hold up one work in the social sciences from the last decade that succeeded in engaging the public with a seemingly coherent body of research, the choice would be easy but dismaying. Richard Herrnstein and Charles Murray's *The Bell Curve*, published in 1994, was a public and professional sensation. The book, which describes how IQ is the most reliable if much-maligned guide to what is best and most worthy of support in America, was featured on TV's "Nightline" show and sold in K-Mart.[24] Despite its 800-plus pages, heavily footnoted and appendixed, the book spent months on the best-seller lists, all the while garnering strongly critical and laudatory magazine feature stories. Certainly, the liberal press, including the *New Republic*, *New York Times*, and even *Scientific American*, rose as one to denounce its flawed use of IQ, its Republican advocacy, and even, I am afraid, its popularity.[25]

So assured was I by the vehement criticism of it as worse than wrong-headed that I did not read it at the time. In turning to it now, to understand how an Automata Data would handle a controversial work such as this one, I was surprised by how good it is at what I have wanted to do with this project of improving the public value of the social sciences. I cannot recall having read anything in the social sciences that works so hard and skillfully at presenting what the authors believe is a valuable and overlooked source of social science insight. The book has a gentle, take-you-by-the-hand quality usually associated with student-friendly textbooks for undergraduates. It warns readers that difficult or unpleasant concepts are ahead; it prepares them for complicated calculations; it allows for different depths of inquiry by offering chapter summaries, extended footnotes, statistical tables, and even a short stats course in an appendix.

Herrnstein, a Harvard professor of psychology who died a few months before the book was released, and Murray, a writer on social and policy issues, build their case for the life-determining force of IQ on what they declare to be our inescapable need to assess the differences among people, with intelligence the critical factor in all walks of social life, from education to motherhood, with no small implications for public policy.[26] But make no mistake, Herrnstein and Murray use IQ to update a two-century-old race science, making it this century's version of craniometry (although unfortunately judging the races by their skull size did survive until well into this century).

The fallacies of this race science have been exposed time and again, perhaps best in Stephen Jay Gould's *The Mismeasure of Man*; and Gould has certainly figured among the strongest critics of *The Bell Curve*.[27] And while Herrnstein and Murray declare themselves "agnostic" on the degree to which IQ is inherited, their every policy initiative would ensure that much of the status quo in this society's racial divisions, the status quo of the 1960s in many cases, would be inherited by future generations.[28] Their book can seem much like a rearguard action, at a time when the white dominance of America may well feel threatened by changing demographics of immigration and birth rates.

Whatever IQ owes to nurture and nature, Herrnstein and Murray argue that this mental capacity can only be improved in individuals by the most radical and unrealistic of measures, such as adoption. This follows from the definition of IQ as a stable quality, with the tests designed to uphold that premise. As a result of this fixed capacity that is held to determine one's place in the world of school, work, and criminal justice, what are traditionally seen as social problems in need of solutions by concerned liberals are reframed as simply the raw facts of nature. Given that, Herrnstein and Murray recommend that we nurture the already gifted and write off the rest, or as they put it in one of the more dour moments in the book: "For many people, there is nothing they can learn that will repay the cost of teaching."[29] Having decided that little can be done, they pose two options for the mental underclass: either contain them in an increasingly "custodial state," or incorporate them within a humane neighborhood governed by a yesteryear vision of swift, firm justice meted out by an unfettered cognitive elite.

Allow me to leave their chilling conclusion unchallenged, that I might face the larger question *The Bell Curve* poses for an Automata Data: does the Corporation represent such work as falling within the domain of knowledge the social sciences have to offer the public? This boils down to whether IQ is a valid measure on which to base social science research. Would there be grounds for excluding such findings from an Automata Data? Herrnstein and Murray justify their reliance on IQ by claiming it represents "an important and valued trait about people" reflecting "a general capacity for inferring and applying relationships drawn from experience."[30] On the other hand, Stephen Jay Gould holds that IQ "cannot have inherent reality, for it emerges in the form of a mathematical representation for correlations among tests and disappears (or greatly attenuates) in other forms, which are entirely equivalent in amount of information explained."[31] Which is to say that intelligence, and its associated behaviors, can be thought of as other than a singular and fixed measure. Gould offers the example of the multiple intelligences theory, currently championed by Howard Gardner and first espoused by J. P. Guilford in the 1950s. Interestingly enough, such an argument does not totally undermine IQ. While it may be but one of many ways of handling different test results, people may still prefer it over others, which is Herrnstein and Murray's populist point and part of its claim as public knowledge.

Herrnstein and Murray find their warrant for supporting a singular, stable, and unmistakable quality known as intelligence in a rather sweeping summary of human history: "Literate cultures everywhere and throughout history have had words for saying that some people are smarter than others" is how they put it squarely on page one of *The Bell Curve*, and all follows from this premise. They leap from assuming a cultural universal in the word for "smarter than others" to a belief in a singular and stable quality of smartness that can be measured. Putting a specific number on this quality of smartness was initiated by Charles Spearman in 1904 when he developed his calculations for *g* as a scientific approximation of this oft-identified smartness factor.

Given that Herrnstein and Murray are playing to the crowd, this claim of popular support for IQ begs its own form of research. (People could be asked about their perception of the stability of their own intelligences, which for many of us can often appear to fluctuate over the course of a morning. Then there is the instability of IQ scores, which have been rising about three points a decade for some time.)[32] Such research is the sort of work, you can foresee me saying, of an Automata Data. It would also be the place to address such concerns as the one raised by University of Michigan psychologist Richard Nisbett, that "almost all of the direct evidence has been left out" on the genetic contribution to racial differences in IQ.[33] All of this points, in my estimation, to the inclusion of the work on IQ, as well as the challenges to it, as part of the resources Automata Data would make available. The Automata Data web site would offer access to the original data as well as to related research through a range of categories, including intelligence, academic differences, racial differences, gifted education, affirmative action, psychological testing, and perhaps "*The Bell Curve* controversy."

The web site's handling of the topic of affirmative action, for example, could include, among a wide range of studies on the subject, Murray and Herrnstein's case on the policy's failure, with links to the critiques of that part of their argument, as well as to their book as a whole. It would include continuously updated data on enrollments at key education and employment institutions. It would invite commentary on the issue, tracking the changing responses to the situation and the research. It could include, for example, the change of heart experienced by sociologists Nathan Glazer and William Julius Wilson, who after effectively arguing against any form of special preference have now qualified their arguments and found ways of supporting these measures, just as, in response to the impact in California, a number of states are now moving away from proposed anti-affirmative action legislation.[34] Automata Data would do well to represent how those working in the social sciences are given to reflecting on changing circumstances, and are prepared to rethink their position in response.

I would not want to minimize the labor and controversy involved in even approaching a fair representation of controversial issues. Automata Data would be the first to point out to users the limits of its compressed point-and-click environment, while experimenting with different ways of organizing and presenting information. But that in itself, that finding of new ways to order and arrange what the social sciences know, is an important step for this field to take. One hope is that by juxtaposing and linking the range of social science inquiry that bears on this policy initiative, we would make it that much easier to see what research would further clarify, resolve, test, or extend our understanding of how this policy works.

While Automata Data would not serve as a Supreme Court of the Social Sciences offering decisive rulings (or dissenting briefs), it would cultivate a site for weighing the evidence and arguments on social science issues such as intelligence, as well as on the social policy front, where the social sciences are invoked.[35] It would encourage debate around a work such as Thomas Sowell's *The Vision of the Anointed: Self-Congratulation as a Basis for Social*

Policy, in which this sharp-tongued social analyst can barely contain his contempt for the liberal vision of society and its flagrant disregard and abuse of social science research. "The vision prevailing among the intellectual and political elite of our time," Sowell writes, is "so much taken for granted by so many people, including so-called 'thinking people,' that neither those assumptions nor their corollaries are generally confronted with demands for empirical evidence."[36] And on he runs, revealing what he sees as the lack of "factual evidence and logical arguments" behind the war on poverty, justice and health reforms, and other "crusades of the anointed."[37] He trots out the figures to show that where liberals fight crime, crime goes up, and where they seek to assist the poor, then more people go poor. He is obviously not above suggesting he has found a *cause* where he should know better with statistics. The reasons for poverty are more complicated than his own self-congratulation allows, which is why we need a way to move beyond the mutual condescension. What seems a far better course is for both sides to come together over the available data, that we might better judge what the social sciences offer in making sense of this world.[38]

I certainly support Sowell's call for a testing of the consequences of differing beliefs on reducing poverty and dependency, especially where goals are shared across a wide political spectrum.[39] While I would not want to underestimate the challenges of bringing social scientists of very different persuasions together to compare their analysis and data, such "antithetical collaboration" would offer its own intellectual interest, as well as new challenges in representing how one study articulates with another in a readily comprehensible way. Judging by the relish Sowell brings to his attack, it will not be easy for polemicists to give up broad-siding each other, and the resulting calm may seem a little dull by comparison. But in support of such sport, *The National Review* will still, I'm sure, go head-to-head with *The Nation* over welfare, affirmative action, or the justice system. The difference with Automata Data will be that readers can follow the hyperlinks to check the facts for themselves, and the writers may have to be a mite more careful knowing that readers' access to the data is only a click away.

One area where social science research has perhaps its greatest impact on the public, and one which I have yet to consider, is with those massive sections of undergraduate students sitting in university lecture theaters, their fluorescently highlighted social science textbooks before them on the minidesks, while the professor entertains them with the fundamentals of social analysis. Such situations can become the perfect meeting ground of public and scholarly concern, especially around an issue like family values that can pit the social sciences against popular conservative opinion.

A study commissioned by the Institute of American Values has recently leveled serious charges of misrepresentation in undergraduate sociology textbooks regarding the current well-being of the modern family. Conducted by Norval Glenn, a sociologist at the University of Texas at Austin, the study purports that most textbooks present a less than friendly picture of the family and, more seriously, are intellectually flawed by their tendency to draw on a single 1973 study—Jessie Bernard's *The Future of Marriage*, which portrays the institution as costly for women in stress and depression. The commissioning of Glenn's study may well reflect the success Stephanie Coontz, a sociologist at Evergreen University, has had in bringing the social sciences to bear on this public debate about the need to restore family values. On the Oprah Winfrey show, among other places, Coontz has effectively exposed how the picture painted by family-values advocates is about "the way we never were." Riddling the hollow nostalgia of this movement, she demands that they name the year of that familial paradise.

For his part, Glenn accuses textbooks like Arlene Skolnick's *The Intimate Environment* of bordering on "educational malpractice" in their failure to address fully the consequences of divorce for children. Glenn recommends peer review for textbooks, although this would not solve the problem because, given his findings, authors can find plenty of peers who would endorse what Glenn finds irresponsible in these works. On reviewing the social science debate on the family, Alan Wolfe, a Boston University sociologist, allows that this may be one of those questions for which both sides are able to find strong supporting evidence, although he leans toward research on the contribution made by traditional families to the well-being of individuals, leading him to conclude that this, "among our most vulnerable citizens, may be just what the doctor ordered."[40]

In a case such as the status of the family, Automata Data's guide to the schools of thought and research would do well to demonstrate how the knowledge of the family divides itself across political lines, not just to dispel the myths about the family that do not stand up to the empirical data, but to demonstrate how the social sciences reflect the edgy democratic pluralism evoked by such fundamental issues as how people choose to live together. Automata Data's presentation of the research in this way would likely attract much commentary and many challenges to which it would be linked, just as the web site would lead into related policy and legal dimensions, as well as, perhaps, to literary and other creative representations of the modern state of the family. Funding for Automata Data's coverage of the family would probably represent a similar diversity of viewpoints, including the Institute of American Values as well as more progressive agencies, with measures obviously in place to ensure that this support did not skew the overall presentation of the current state of research, as well as the range of studies commissioned or coordinated through Automata Data.

Given Glenn's critique of the undergraduate textbook, Automata Data's coverage could also be designed to enable students to move from the often smoothed-over textbook presentation of research to the rough contest of ideas in real life, while including opportunities to reanalyze the data and weigh the claims. The students could as easily work from the primary data, such as the National Longitudinal Survey of Youth, as with a commentary, such as Wolfe's, on the state of the research. The educational function of Automata Data, which I introduced earlier, would also prepare a new generation of citizens to be adept at digging among databases, at comparing surveys and narrative research on various issues. It would introduce them to social science research's engagement with public values, as well as their own rights, responsibilities, and potential contributions to this academic generation of knowledge. Students could review the efforts of social scientists from various disciplines and persuasions to produce helpful bodies of information and understanding on a phenomenon of which, in the case of the family certainly, they have firsthand knowledge themselves. This puts them in a position to review and critique the very setup of Automata Data's site as as a source of public understanding on a topic such as the state of the family. They could lend their own weight to the call for further studies of what is, to them, clearly missing in the social sciences' efforts to grasp the contribution and challenges posed by this fundamental social structure.

I should perhaps pause here, amid the slightly heady prospect of students participating in this knowledge process, to allow that exposure to this social science research and scholarship may not change very many minds. Those who are undecided on any given issue are always small in number, just as are those who are truly open to the force of argument and information. Among these, it might seem, Automata Data stands to make its greatest democratic and educational contribution. Otherwise, it offers the already converted the comfort and specification of confirming studies, even as it provides a larger context of consequences that surround that position. In this way an Automata Data could raise the level of debate, by at least suggesting that opposing views are not without their reasons; and that debate, in turn, could prompt the extension and testing of related assumptions.

You may have noted, perhaps gratefully, that up to this point I have let all talk of technology, apart from references to the web site, slip from view. This is, of course, consistent with my belief that this project of renewing the social contract of the social sciences is not about technology, but a determination, a determination to use whatever tools are available to do a better job of creating a public resource out of the research enterprise. Still, I cannot close this chapter on democracy without recognizing the enthusiasm for how certain forms of technology can develop new levels of public engagement and community, in a coda that offers its own resistant notes from the underground within the new networked age of information.

Online Coda

The global network that has sprung up around the Internet does suggest a new world order, with every user in front of every terminal granted equal access, immediate and direct, to the public screen, especially for speakers of English. Who has not been impressed with the bureaucracy-defeating qualities of this great communication equalizer? After China opened global Internet connections in 1994, dissidents and others interested in social change in China quickly began using elaborate redistribution systems to circumvent state censorship of critical political information that supported the democracy movement.[41] When it comes to the democratic future for knowledge, a phone jack and a computer do appear to be one ticket, and if most of the world has yet to make its first phone call, it may be reassuring to know that the voice at the other end will ask, when they do make that initial modem call, "Where do you want to go today?"—to borrow the question trademarked by Microsoft. With so much information and political activity already available on the web, I may be way off in imagining that our political futures have something to gain by the social sciences creating through Automata Data a vast public resource of accumulated and varied wisdom on the web.

The best known of the network's alternative politics is found through WELL (Whole Earth 'Lectronic Link), which is an electronic bulletin board service that originated in the Bay Area of San Francisco that dates back to 1985. As participant and writer Howard Rheingold tells it, the WELL stands as part of, in his words, an "alternative planetary information system."[42] Once there was the *Whole Earth Catalog*, which had many of us believing we could shop our way out of the 'burbs of the 1950s and into the Age of Aquarius. Now there is the "electronic agora" of the WELL online in a marketplace of free-flowing talk and people, after the agora of ancient Greece and the founding of democracy. Here people gather to chat and challenge each other, to support and nurture, to create knowing, alternative communities around an array of shared interests within the categories of Arts and Letters, Recreation, Education and Planning, and the Grateful Dead. They also meet in real life. These communities of interest signal for Rheingold the emergence of a new public space, a commons, that has otherwise been lost to suburbs and cocooning. It does awaken dreams of that youthful alternative culture of our boomer yesteryears, given to communes and communing. He casts it as a source of genuine discourse; it is, after all, devoid of advertising.[43]

This building of online communities, in both a local and a global sense, does have a part to play in how we understand the future of knowledge, representing a distributed knowing or collective wisdom that builds with successive exchanges of email. It represents a non-automata means of thinking through issues in the company of others, rather than under anyone's tutelage, with the exchange gradually forming its own database on the topic. The WELL exemplifies how a technology can be turned to democratic ends, and I would not want to lose sight of that achievement.[44] The WELL is given to this fostering of community and collective wisdom, while Automata Data, and the social sciences more generally, are committed to pursuing a certain kind of knowledge, in the belief that these technologies of knowing have become necessary to achieving democratic ends within the complex communities we inhabit.

Richard Sclove, founder of FASTnet (Federation of Activists on Science and Technology Network), is another person deeply committed to exploring "the first-order question [that attends to] the structural bearings of technologies on democracy." Those structures can take many forms, not least of which are those through which, in Sclove's words, "people can educate themselves and learn to deliberate together."[45] Now, simply offering online access to a universal citation database of the sort I described earlier will only serve a few of the most dedicated information seekers and surfers. And even then, think of what they would face with a topic such as the research on bilingual education. Something more by way of order and coordination will always be needed.

Such is Automata Data's mission. If it works at all, Automata Data would increase the social sciences' stake as part of the public knowledge that matters, because people will know that they can turn to it as an accessible source of insight and argument. Such would be the Corporation's democratic experiment. Automata Data is all about testing whether the social sciences are prepared to a better job of delivering on the Kantian promise of delivering justice and equality in the name of a reason that can move people out from under the undue tutelage and direction of others. As this Enlightenment contraption of a corporation I am proposing wobbles and perhaps stalls along this highway of reason, it will at least have the advantage of then transforming itself into a critique of this persistent dream of reason's benefit and knowledge's democratic contribution.

8

Knowledge Futures

THE AUTOMATA DATA CORPORATION amounts to an experiment in the public value of a certain kind of knowledge. More specifically, it is about the difference that might come of improving public access to social science research. It is intended to test what I have been calling the public value of the social sciences, by affording social scientists a new way of serving public interests. In its efforts to bring about greater coherence within social science research activities, Automata Data would broker and coordinate research proposals, commission studies and propose standards, establish data pools, and secure data sources. It would create a site on the web designed to improve public access to what the social sciences have to offer, in all of their variety, on a wide range of issues and questions. It would invite debate and dialogue over converging and diverging research strands on given topics. It would continually assess its own contribution as a public utility, in both the Corporation's responsiveness to public interests and its leadership in expanding those interests. It would try to capture the always elusive state of what is possible within the scope of the social sciences, even as that scope changes through this engagement with public knowledge.

This book is not, however, intended to be a business plan for Automata Data disguised in academically sheepish clothing. I have risked an act of social science fiction, with the speculative, slightly alien character of corporate guises and computer gizmos, to give life to otherwise dry questions of how a vast intellectual endeavor can better serve public and practitioner.

When I trotted out my Automata Data in the trial-run laboratory of the professorial dinner party, I found my colleagues at first slightly surprised at the idea, as if unsure that they had heard right. They reacted as though I wanted to fix something that is not broken. If it is still being funded, their polite but inquisitive look suggests, why would I mess with the formula? I reassure them that the tenured momentum of the social sciences will carry our current array of research programs well beyond my own lifetime. And the information will slowly mushroom outward, occasionally generating a little random news and a little public indifference. Against that flow, I explain, my interest is only in seeing how much more *could* be done, with the technologies at hand, to wrest greater public and personal value from all that these related disciplines have made of the world. Having said that, I can feel their sense that there is something disturbingly ambitious, if not megalomaniacal, about this scheme. They are right, and I wince at what one dinner companion called my "scientific pretensions." I may well pretend too much, but not all that much more, perhaps, than the profession I am taking at its word on its commitment to the commonweal. Automata Data sounds like an extreme measure, with its aggravating language of corporation coordination, collaboration, and coherence, but it takes extremes to stake out middle paths.

Within such pretension, Automata Data is but a stepping stone—and one much stepped on, if I am lucky—on the way to reopening the social contract between the public and the social sciences within an economy otherwise devoted to knowledge discovery, production, and utilization. My concern is that if we do not begin consolidating the knowledge at hand in the social sciences, while at the same time increasing the number of public access points to it, our ongoing research efforts will not only operate outside that economy but, by some perverse logic, will only add to that region judged unknowable and mysterious.

When I was younger, the science writer Martin Gardner first made his name (at least in my book) with *Relativity for the Millions*, in all the fascination, frustration, and pleasure he provided while helping the rest of us try to work through what an Einsteinian universe might be about. And it was no easy go, puzzling through the scientific analogies of traveling in elevators and trains that were approaching the speed of light. Presumably, it should be easier to follow different methods of analyzing affirmative action and bilingual education, workfare and immigration, than to comprehend Einstein's special theory of relativity. The advantage of Automata Data is that theoretical physics is unlikely to be improved by this public engagement, whereas the social sciences could learn a good deal from having those studied more interested in the results of this inquiry.

As it stands today, newspapers have been improving their presentation of social science research, most notably in qualifying the reliability of the opinion polls they print. *USA Today* has made colorful *info-graphics* part of its mission, with often quirky social stats on the front page of its various sections. The design challenge for Automata Data will be to integrate the words, numbers, charts, and tables, from a wide range of research methods, to make the individual studies, as well as the relationship among studies, far more accessible and intelligible than is currently the case. It will take the talents of someone like Edward R. Tufte, whom the *New York Times* calls the "da Vinci of data." Tufte, a professor of political science at Yale, is able "to turn seas of information into navigable—even scenic—waterways," as demonstrated through his beautiful best-sellers *Envisioning Information* and *Visual Explanations.*[1] In cultivating public access to the social sciences, Automata Data will obviously place new demands on researchers as both writers and educators, challenging them to rethink their craft and talent in ways that may ultimately draw them further into the public sphere.

One relevant and current experiment in public access is the quarterly *DoubleTake*, edited by Robert Cole, professor of social ethics at Harvard. Published by the Center for Documentary Studies at Duke University, *DoubleTake* offers a newsstand model of how the social sciences, humanities, literature, and photography can come together in a form and with a circulation (about 55,000) that can draw advertising dollars from Absolut Vodka. Its commitment is to portraying, as Cole puts it, "aspects of a troubled nation's social reality" while managing, through the shared sensibilities of poets, photographers, and ethnographers, to do "compelling justice to what they heard and witnessed."[2] *DoubleTake*'s very use of the camera is a reminder of how technologies can be turned to uniting purposes and transcending boundaries of disciplines and arts, in the name of a compelling justice.

What Cole is achieving, and I am proposing on a much larger

scale, is no more than to make good on an old and oft-repeated promise that haunts the social sciences. Some thirty years ago, Edward Shils, a sociologist at the University of Chicago and Cambridge, expressed his hope that sociology would be nothing less than "a constituent of public rationality." He saw it contributing to "the extension and elevation of the public life of society by improving the citizen's understanding of the collective life in which he is involved and improving the quality of discussion among citizens." Shils was making a thoroughly Kantian appeal to a sociology that "leaves to the human beings to whom it is addressed the freedom of interpretation and judgment which is needed in the public life of a reasonably decent [and, he might have added, democratic] society."[3] On their own, sociology and the other social sciences have yet to fully realize that constituent role in the play of public reason, and it represents a loss for the social sciences and for democracy. Something more needs to be tried, I am obviously persuaded, given that the social sciences otherwise risk being part of an ill-fated economic cycle of information explosion and exasperation.

In the field of education, the public has most recently been interested in what research has to say about computers in the classroom, while already sounding rightfully disappointed with the preliminary results. There is considerable public and political support for the use of technology in the schools, but the opportunity appears about to be squandered for want of some straight answers on why and how these machines should be used. I am among those who have produced small-scale studies in this line, with my work on the positive gains made by students who used computers to expand the audience they wrote for and, more recently, by students who turned computers into an opportunity to help others.[4] But these positive studies sit with others, or rather against others, at least one of which was also mine, in which computer-using students demonstrated no gains, except in the length of their writing.[5] And, as we saw with bilingual education, the studies have a way of quickly canceling each other out.

Certainly Todd Oppenheimer has concluded as much in his controversial *Atlantic Monthly* essay, "The Computer Delusion."[6] Oppenheimer is unequivocal in claiming that there is simply no good reason to believe at this point that computers are helping in the classroom. By reason, he means research. Without the research to back it up, the computer in the classroom risks being labeled an educational fad and written off as the filmstrip of the 1990s. While I would happily enter the fray over technology and education—beginning with how filmstrips were hardly the commonplace tool of the workplace that computers are—I leave such rebuttals for another time and place. Here I only want to point out that for all intents and purposes the research community appears to be doing it all over again.

Public exasperation is already apparent over what research might offer on the topic. "The research [on the educational value of computers] is set up in a way to find benefits that aren't really there," states Edward Miller, a former editor of the *Harvard Education Letter* and one of Oppenheimer's key expert witnesses on the great delusion. "Most knowledgeable people agree that most of the research isn't really valid. It's so flawed it shouldn't even be called research. Essentially, it's just worthless."[7] He invites us to join him in shaking our collective heads over this failure of knowledge. Although Miller is clearly given to sweeping and unsubstantiated statements, much as he would accuse others of doing, there is no mistaking that it is difficult to discover what all the research on computers and learning adds up to, or how it sorts itself out at this point.

For his part, Oppenheimer attributes the lack of "solid conclusions" about the benefits of computers to the sheer ineffectiveness of the machines in helping students to learn, combined with the corrupting influence of industry sponsorship of the research. Something is seriously amiss within the social sciences when the work of major National Science Foundation research projects, as well as dozens of academic journals, all assembling information on the impact of technology on education, can be so summarily dismissed as worthless if not actually tainted. I am sure that each of the studies can be demonstrated to have its own integrity, its own contribution to make, its own critical analysis of what to expect from this influx of technology. Where does one turn to gain a sense of the whole of this work, to assess where the technology works and where it fails? Where can one register an interest in having certain research questions answered that might guide educational policies in this area?

Encouraging signs of change in this dismal state of affairs are beginning to light the horizon. For example, in 1997, when the President's Committee of Advisers on Science and Technology proposed that $1.5 billion dollars be spent on researching technology's place in education, Senator Jeff Bingaman and others were ready to insist that this be done only through the coordinating efforts of a national consortium of business concerns, higher education, research institutes, and government.[8] Just another excuse, you may well imagine, for scheduling meetings and building bureaucratic empires. Still, it speaks to an interest in improving the public value of the social sciences, which I obviously feel the research community should pursue.

Impetus Redux

As I have already suggested, Automata Data is not so much a stunningly original idea as a gentle push in the direction of a number of existing efforts. This is fortunate for me, because if the idea were new it would have far less chance of provoking even passing consideration. Elements of what Automata Data would do to bring greater order to the social sciences are already underway, whether in a research index such as ERIC or in Evidence-Based Medicine; in sophisticated but not infallible procedures for the meta-analysis of multiple studies; in systematic reviews of the research on specific topics. Automata Data, a hyperlinked hybrid of encyclopedia, library, and database, is one way existing initiatives can be adapted to make greater public and common sense of the field.

I have played down the theme of automation within Automata Data, but it is all about simplifying and electrifying the connections among data, ideas, and people. The links among them are automated not in a futuristic sense, but much like our phones and faxes are automated systems with machines making the connections for us rather than people. Equally so, the world of data is already heavily automated, as it is collected, processed, and distributed. Automata Data would only seek bring that much more of this data work into the service of a vital public sector. Information may want to be free, as the net-anarchists hold, but it may take a corporation to make information publicly accessible when it comes to working on the scale of social science research—a corporation for public knowledge.

One consequence of the pragmatic approach I am proposing for Automata Data—which denies it the dream of achieving a unified body of social science knowledge or even a foundation of certain irrefutable truths—is that people will be disappointed, at least initially, by the Corporation's steadfast refusal to pronounce winners and losers, to champion bilingual education and denounce IQ, or vice versa. There will be no promises of conclusive results held out, pending further studies and fresh data. No story of unfolding research progress on the road, thanks to Automata Data, to convergence and consensus within the social sciences. And yet no flinching at asking researchers to respond to studies that appear to undermine any claim their posted work might have to social science. Automata Data would, in the name of coherence, seek to resolve differences of technique, discrepancies of measure, disagreements of category, so that the values at stake could become readily comprehensible points of public judgment. The comprehension and coherence of this fundamental plurality is the core of this democratic project with knowledge. Providing access to the arguments and data for and against a work such as Herrnstein and Murray's *The Bell Curve* is the very point of an Automata Data. Such would be its faith in the social sciences as a line of reasoning.

Certainly, the research posted by Automata Data will continue the tradition of concluding with specific recommendations that presumably follow logically from their findings. Studies will still take strong stances, advocate and argue positions. All that would change is that researchers would have greater incentive to state the risks and possibilities associated with their recommendations in ways that enable comparison with other studies and factors, if only because of the virtual proximity of those studies. In this way, Automata Data's peer-review screening of the research will not only be aimed at the traditional concerns of research rigor, but will help authors situate their work for a wider public.

Yet apart from this review process, Automata Data will resist putting its own stamp of approval on the practices and policies recommended by the individual and collective studies and commentaries posted. It will not feature a five-star ranking system for research or offer a Research Pick-o'-the-Week. (But wait, you may want to warn me, until Automata Data's marketing people explain to me the price of pursuing public interests.) The goal will remain, however, that enlightening environment in which public feel encouraged and supported in finding their own way and drawing their own conclusions. This is not to deny that Automata Data's very presentation of the research will inevitably influence how it is received. This topic will be the subject of much discussion and experimentation. It would be part of what I imagine as a larger process of participation between profession and public that addresses gaps in coverage, queries confusions and challenges contradictions in the representation, approaches, and areas of inquiry of the studies posted.

Automata Data would only accept commissions for new studies from individuals, commercial interests, not-for-profits, and government agencies under terms that would support further access to its services by disadvantaged individuals and groups. Automata Data would itself commission studies, largely directed at improving the cumulative value of existing work. It would help broker ongoing studies that mined commercial and government data sources. It would coordinate and manage large-scale multidimensional studies, as well as assist in setting international standards for data collection to facilitate the integration of findings on a global scale.

This theme of globalization would pose a special challenge to Automata Data, as it does to the social sciences in general.[9] The social sciences have for too long been national projects content to assume that such boundaries continue to define the relevant world. That is why we have anthropology and comparative sociology for venturing abroad. It will take some doing to broaden perspectives in the social sciences to match the global scale of other sectors of this knowledge economy. One point of caution has been offered by the sociologist Pablo González Casanova, who concluded a number of years ago that international social science projects were actually undermined by careful adherence to singular research designs, usually dictated by the researchers at the dominant institutions. These studies had the effect of excluding locally developed, alternative hypotheses; they lost the value of regional differences and the very benefits of collaboration on a global basis.[10] Within the methodological eclecticism of Automata Data, it should not be too much to collectively work out research design standards and variations, which would allow researchers to present global patterns, while developing regional variations, in an ongoing dynamic within the circulation of local initiatives and global themes that information technologies are often credited with fostering.

My fear is that efforts to renew the social contract between social sciences and public could be taken up as another way for America to strengthen its democracy, intellectually enrich its citizens, and improve its social systems, as if its gift to the world were always to take careful of itself, as becomes a supermodel. The social sciences clearly have a great deal to learn about knowledge as a cooperative resource, just as we need to conceive of this research's public value on a global basis. This will follow from its increasing engagement with the new world system of capitalism, especially in studies of the media and global cultural influences, as well as from assessing the impact of new trade patterns, global divisions of labor and working conditions, and immigration trends.[11] New global data is needed in such areas as family households, given current inabilities, for example, to accurately track women's health in relation to other family members.[12] This knowledge on a global scale will need to be directed not only at assisting social scientists in developing a more complete picture, but at assisting local social movements, democratic initiatives, and educational innovations. It will take time to check the social science tendency to think of knowledge as radiating out from what was once the West. So the English language is bound to continue to dominate the research presented by Automata Data, with forms of automated translation only very slowly improving. Global access would become another issue for Automata Data, which could join in the push for the World Bank and other organizations to fund greater access to the Internet, just as it might work closely with the social science activities of UNESCO.[13] And to the raise the issue of the United Nations is, at the very least, to introduce the matter of funding and how the particular knowledge economy of an Automata Data might operate.

I have not spent much time on the financial viability of a corporation for public knowledge such as Automata Data. The question seems to me secondary to the critical initial step of renewing the principles of the social sciences' social contract. I did touch on the relatively minor concern of reducing research costs when I alluded to how people, once convinced of the value of the research, might well agree to release encrypted forms of their medical or educational records to a data-miner run by Automata Data. Not only would the resulting research speak that much more accurately to their own situation, it might well be treated as a tax write-off for data contributors, comparable to donating books to a library. I can also imagine commercial operations donating, for similar tax concessions, the transaction data they keep. And of course, the encryption systems would allow data from various sources to be matched up.[14]

However, before fussing over spreadsheet projections of cash and data flow, we need to think about how to assess the larger worth of this project. With an understanding of where Automata Data fits in the knowledge economy, as a public/private not-for-profit, we can talk about how specific aspects of it should be funded. That may seem like a typical academic dodge of fiscal responsibility. But I would propose that Automata Data could improve the place of the social sciences within a knowledge economy like this: Begin with the idea that, as things now stand, the public is receiving a certain value from its investment in social science research. Let us then assume as a starting point for any calculations that we are working with the following formula: current *public investment in research* (PIR) equals the current *public value of research* (PVR), or PIR = PVR. That is, whatever value the research now has for the public, its cost amounts to the current public investment in that research.

This public investment takes the form of direct funding for research from governments and foundations, as well as university support of faculty members and graduate students for that portion of their time devoted to research, with the funds coming from tuition, government grants, and endowments. I would wildly hazard that the public investment in social science research might reach as high as to $3–4 billion annually.[15] But the figure itself is not important. The issue is whether the social sciences can, through an organization like Automata Data, improve the public value of the knowledge they produce at current levels of funding. The Corporation would compete for grants and would be commissioned to conduct studies. It might also charge researchers a fee for brokering data and information from various sources. The majority of Automata Data's revenue would be spent on designing, building, and maintaining the public utility web site to capture the current state of knowledge in the social sciences. This would, in effect, remove existing funding from the support of additional studies.

This would alter the original formula of PIR = PVR. With the funding of the Automata Data Corporation (ADC) drawn from the public investment in research, the formula would now read: PIR − ADC = PVR. That is, the funds going into Automata Data Corporation would be subtracted from the public investment in research, *per se*. Since this would reduce the number of studies conducted, Automata Data's only justification for doing so would be to increase *public value of research* (PVR). So the question of whether Automata Data is financially viable would go something like this: Would both the public and the social sciences get a better return on the current investment in research by funding the operating budget for Automata Data (perhaps 0.5 percent of the public investment in social science research, providing it with an annual budget of perhaps a $15–25 million)?

If Automata Data were to create a 20 percent improvement in the public value of social science research, the formula would then look like this: 1.2(PIR − ADC) = PVR (compared to the current PIR = PVR). What would a 20 percent improvement in the public value of research (PVR) look like? Given the current public value of research, it would not take too much. Automata Data would have to demonstrate a 20 percent increase in the number of people who turned to social science research for assistance in thinking through and possibly acting on an issue; or the government saw a 20 percent increase in the number of studies consulted in arriving at a policy proposal; or the cost of gathering data for studies, as well as the subsequent cost of the meta-studies to pull those studies together, was cut by 20 percent through co-ordinated and automated strategies of an Automata Data.[16]

I do not want to get too carried away with this speculative eco-nomic algebra. Let us just say that the cost-benefit analysis of an Automata Data Corporation depends on whether the increased public value of social science research proves noticeably greater than any loss of direct investment in research studies. I do not want to be flip about the value of yet another research project, and not just because it could be one of my projects we are talking about. But I do think that the financing of an Automata Data lies within the realm of what is economically feasible given existing fiscal arrangements, even as it would strengthen the social sci-ences' very claim to continuing public support.[17] And as I have already suggested that the idea for this corporation be tested first within a given topic area, its financing would also be tested on a small scale—perhaps following the model of the Corporation for Public Broadcasting, which was initially seeded as a trial by the major foundations.

I am less certain about how Automata Data would affect the knowledge economy of journals and academic publishing in gen-eral, once it was fully underway. It could be that Automata Data would assume responsibility for peer-reviewing much of the work intended to serve public and practitioner, as well as re-searchers. There is certainly a lot of interest in reforming current journal-publishing practices. The International Coalition of Li-brary Consortia has recently issued a concerned statement on the current "electronic information environment." The statement speaks of a "scholarly communication system that is becoming dysfunctional" with symptoms including an increasing volume of redundant and repetitive journal publication for tenure and promotion certification. They call for "disincentives for unnecessary publication," and perhaps more realistically, for libraries, authors, publishers, and universities "to take risks to create and implement new, technologically enabled research outlets for initial publication of scholarship and research results."[18]

Scholars may well find a real sense of intellectual accomplishment in organizing and coordinating the coverage of different topics for Automata Data, much as they do in assembling the massive surveys of the research handbooks reviewed earlier. They may also be drawn into developing and researching new techniques of presentation, as well as assessing the public impact and value of different forms of knowledge. There is no way of guessing how the actual writing—the presentation of data and analysis—would change in response to not only the electronic medium, but the change of purpose and the interactive and immediate juxtaposition of ideas. The academic essay has held its own through the centuries, with slight variations from one discipline to the next. The constant had been the medium of the printed page, and it appears that print may soon cease to be the dominant form of delivery for scholarly publication. An Automata Data would certainly press for far more precise and standardized abstracts, following the model of the health sciences. But I do not want to be caught out predicting the future. Suffice it to say that there would be much experimentation on the possibilities of the medium, and much resistance to change.

The critical factor here is not the new medium. As I have repeatedly stated, change will come only if those working in the social sciences decide that it would be a good idea to organize a far more helpful resource for public and practitioners, for agencies and individuals. Do we want to provide more for those facing difficult decisions, formulating policies, or looking for a way forward? Those who work in the social sciences might well be drawn to the intellectual challenge of constructing better ways of organizing and presenting the fine distinctions of our work, better ways of representing the limits and confluence of what is known and how it is known. This is no less true for those who reject the number crunching and table building in favor of what can be told through narratives and cases. The social sciences have entered into a social contract to deliver a knowledge that makes greater sense of the social world.

Automata Data is about testing the contribution the social sciences have to make by improving their ability to deliver on its promise. It is not premised on the assumption that this society is headed for ruin if it ignores the lessons the social sciences have to teach, nor that this is the knowledge necessary and sufficient for democratic action. It is simply about assessing whether this peculiar form of knowledge could do more, as knowledge, for the people in whose name it is pursued.

To bring this round, finally, to a personal scale, I started out as a school teacher a long time ago because it seemed a way to share with people what was itself the public good of ideas, places, books, numbers, games. When that occupation was not exactly producing the amount of good that I had imagined it would—whether totally through my own failings as a teacher or those of the school, I was not sure—I turned to the social sciences to better understand why education was not working out better for all of the students with whom I was working. Through graduate studies in education, I edged my way into the ranks of those producing articles of explanation and understanding of educational processes. In the process of my becoming a professor of education, a door closed behind me. I found myself within a research community dedicated to these articles of faith in the social sciences, a community to whom I now pose this challenge of working through new technologies and old frustrations in renewing our social contract with public and practitioners. Automata Data seems to me a particularly social science response to the question of fulfilling a public trust, although it seems to me equally important to protect the right to work outside it. I am only trying to imagine some way to make this improvement of the public and democratic value of our work plausible and perhaps tempting.

What I have made of the social sciences, without undue exaggeration I hope, is an earnest field, deeply engaged in research, that from helicopter height at least appears in some disarray. Efforts to bring to it greater order are underway, although these seem to work best at assisting the research community rather than the public or the practicing professional. I am tempted to regard meta-analysis, meta-indexes and meta-reviews as after-the-fact concessions that something needs to be done about the lack of coordination in organizing our research efforts, rather than as a concerted effort at improving the public value of this professional knowledge. So I risk the indignant insistence that an Automata Data will kill off the uninhibited process of discovery, the serendipitous and follow-your-instinct fury, which alone can deliver the big breakthroughs in knowledge we so desperately need. If only such serendipity and fury were what all the social sciences were about. Even allowing for that handful of independent souls who need untrammeled freedom to know where no one has known before, there is still plenty of room for improving the coordination among research programs, and building a public space for sharing what the social sciences have to offer.

The social sciences are only rarely about data-driven or conceptual breakthroughs. For most of us involved in the daily work of this knowledge trade, the social sciences are about belaboring a handful of carefully applied methods in hopes of assembling a little more of what can be known about the risks and possibilities people face as they try to make greater sense of their lives. We operate on public trust, constantly seeking the new grounds and grace necessary for prying into people's lives in the name of some greater good of knowing. Whatever our method, we have produced an immense body of disparate knowledge for which I am convinced that greater order and value can be found. We need only consider how we might better serve those we would study, to experiment with new forms and ways of realizing the good we imagine this knowledge doing. Through this book you have entered the imaginary confines of an initial dry run for this project. That only leaves me now to ask, how did it work for you? What do you make of it? What do you want to do about it?

http://www.knowarch.com/automata.data

Notes

Chapter 1: Random News

1. Reprinted in the *New York Times*, 27 April 1997, E4.
2. *Globe & Mail*, 1 June 1998, A5.
3. Stephen G. Pauker, "Contentious Screening Decisions: Does the Choice Matter?" *New England Journal of Medicine* 336, no. 17 (24 April 1997).
4. Abigail Zuger, "Breast Self-Exams Save Lives? Science Still Doesn't Have Answer," *New York Times*, 6 January 1998, B1, B15. The issue is all the more urgent with the incidence of breast cancer rising by close to 2 percent a year, even as mortality rates have declined slightly. Genetic and environmental causes have been identified in roughly a third of the cases, with the rest unknown.
5. Zuger, "Breast Self-Exams."
6. See Suzanne W. Fletcher, "Whither Scientific Deliberations in Health Policy Recommendations? Alice in the Wonderland of Breast-Cancer Screening," *New England Journal of Medicine* 336, no. 17 (17 April 1997) for a review of the reception of the conclusion reached by a "consensus-development panel" convened by the National Institute of Health. Fletcher argues that the panel's finding, that the "data currently available do not warrant a universal recommendation for mammography" in women age 40–49, was deliberately ignored by policy makers and politicians who came out in support of this procedure.
7. Jane Gadd, "Disease Survivors Mobilize," *Globe & Mail*, 23 June 1997, A1.
8. National Library of Medicine, October 1997, http://text.nlm.nih.gov/. For a discussion of setting up a National Education Library on this model, see

T. Brandhorst, "What Are the Possibilities for Coordinating Education Information Data Bases?" *Knowledge: The International Journal of Knowledge
Transfer* 3, no. 2 (1990).

9. Sheryl Gay Stolberg, "Now, Prescribing Just What the Patient Ordered,"
New York Times, 10 August 1997, E3. A recent poll reports that 60 percent of
women "get most of their medical information" from the media, while
only 13 percent rely on their doctors. Janet Elder, "Poll Finds Women Are
the Health-Savvier Sex, and Warier," *New York Times*, 22 June 1997, WH8.

10. Boston Women's Health Book Collective, *Our Bodies, Ourselves: A Book by
and for Women* (New York: Simon and Schuster, 1973).

11. Thomas Sowell, *Knowledge and Decisions* (New York: Basic Books, 1980).

12. See my *The Empire of Words: The Reign of the OED* (Princeton, N.J.: Princeton University Press, 1994), and *Learning to Divide the World: Education at
Empire's End* (Minneapolis: University of Minnesota Press, 1998).

13. This fictional license seems to be less dangerous and intellectually vulnerable than Immanuel Wallerstein's call to move "utopistics" to the center of
the social sciences. He seeks "the analysis of possible utopias, their limitations and the constraints on achieving them" in a search for goodness rec-
onciled with the search for truth. But then he also sees the social sciences
"as the inevitable ground of a reunited world of knowledge," which is the
dream, as will unfold, to and against which Automata Data speaks. "Social
Science and the Quest for a Just Society," *American Journal of Sociology* 102,
no. 5 (March 1997): 1254, 1256.

14. Borrowed from George Steiner, "Inscrutable and Tragic: Leo Strauss'
Vision of the Jewish Identity," *Times Literary Supplement*, 14 November
1997, 4.

Chapter 2: Corporate Prospects

1. See Morton Keller, "The Making of the Modern Corporation," *Wilson
Quarterly* (autumn 1997): 58–69.

2. Irvin Molotsky, "How One Tough Bird Survived the Attacks on Public
Broadcasting," *New York Times*, 27 November 1997, B1, B14.

3. National Academy of Science, May 1998, http://www2.nas.edu/nas/
211e.html: "The National Academy of Sciences is a private, non-profit, self-
perpetuating society of distinguished scholars engaged in scientific and engineering research, dedicated to the furtherance of science and technology
and to their use for the general welfare. Upon the authority of the charter
granted to it by the Congress in 1863, the Academy has a mandate that re-

quires it to advise the federal government on scientific and technical matters."

4. Kenneth Prewitt, "History of SSRC," December 1997, http://www.ssrc.org/histbri.htm.

5. While the work of PBS is generally well known, Educational Testing Service is less so. Founded in 1947, ETS employs 2,400 people and generates revenues of $400 million through administering 12 million tests a year, from SAT to licensure exams for 34 professions. Because there is no government monitoring of ETS's services, organizations such as the National Center for Fair and Open Testing in Cambridge, Massachusetts have taken on the role of public watchdog. On concerns over ETS's handling of security issues, see Douglas Frantz and Jon Nordheimer, "Giant of Exam Business Keeps Quiet on Cheating," *New York Times*, 28 September 1997, Y1, Y14.

6. Public Agenda, May 1998, http://www.publicagenda.org. Mathematica Policy Research, Inc., May 1998, http://www.mathematica-mpr.com. Rand, May 1998, http://www.rand.org/ABOUT/index.html, describes itself: "Today, RAND researchers operate on a uniquely broad front, assisting public policymakers at all levels, private sector leaders in many industries, and the public at large in efforts to strengthen the nation's economy, maintain its security, and improve its quality of life. They do so by analyzing choices and developments in many areas, including national defense, education and training, health care, criminal and civil justice, labor and population, science and technology, community development, international relations, and regional studies." Mathematica Policy Research, Inc., describes itself as "a leader in policy research and analysis. The firm has conducted some of the most important evaluations of public programs and demonstrations undertaken in the United States. Its studies, which crisscross the human life span from children's health and welfare to long-term care for elderly people, provide a sound foundation for decisions that affect the well-being of Americans. For more than 25 years, the company has offered policymakers a unique combination of evaluation expertise, direct data collection services, and insight into the socioeconomic issues that drive public policy. Its clients include federal agencies, state and local governments, foundations, universities, professional associations, and businesses."

7. As the children's television program narrator in William Gibson's cyberpunk-launching novel, *Neuromancer*, patiently explains, "Cyberspace . . . A consensual hallucination experienced daily by billions of legitimate operators in every nation, by children being taught mathematical concepts . . . . A graphic representation of data abstracted from the banks of every com-

puter in the human system." Gibson, *Neuromancer* (New York: Ace, 1984), 51.

8. Francis Bacon, *The Advancement of Learning and the New Atlantis* (1605; reprint, London: Oxford University Press, 1906).

9. Ibid., 296.

10. Henry Etzkowitz, "The Entrepreneurial University and the Emergence of Democratic Corporatism," in *Universities and the Global Knowledge Economy: A Triple Helix of University-Industry-Government Relations*, ed. Henry Etzkowitz and Loet Leydesdorff (London: Pinter, 1997).

11. Swift adds that the Frame "however might be still improved, and much expedited, if the Public would raise a Fund for making and employing Five Hundred such Frames in Lagado." See *Gulliver's Travels* (New York: Norton, 1970): 152–53, 156. Thanks go to Kieran Egan for this Swiftian poke.

12. "Intel Chairman Remains Confident," *Globe & Mail*, 4 June 1997, B10.

13. Gina Kolata, "Exercise Found to Cut Breast Cancer," *Globe & Mail*, 1 May 1997, A1.

14. Peter T. Kilborn, "Health Gap Grows, With Black Americans Trailing Whites, Studies Say," *New York Times*, 26 January 1998, A16.

15. Lawrence K. Altman, "Studies Show Another Drug Can Prevent Breast Cancer," *New York Times*, 21 April 1998, A16.

16. Former FBI agent John Douglas has complained in the *Wall Street Journal* of how the United States was behind other nations in developing a national computer system to coordinate police case information. His complaint is reprinted in John Douglas and Mark Olshaker, "Getting Away with (Serial) Murder," *Globe & Mail*, 24 July 1997, A17. On the government's concern that encryption will limit its powers, see John Markoff, "Scientists Press Campaign for Computer Data Security," *New York Times*, 24 September 1997, C2. On potato chips, see Jessica Keyes, "The Smart Business," in *Technology Trendlines*, ed. Jessica Keyes (New York: Van Nostrand Reinhold, 1995).

17. The American author Thomas Pynchon, who successfully protected his identity and privacy for forty years, had it all spoiled when *Times* (London) reporter James Bone used Lexis-Nexis, which provides "personal-public information" online, to find Pynchon's New York address. Bruce Culp, "In Search of Thomas Pynchon," *Globe & Mail*, 26 July 1997, D4. Also see Nena Bernstein, "Proposals to Protect Privacy Seem to Face Stalemate in Contradictory Goals," *New York Times*, 20 October 1997, A12.

18. Michael Kesterton, "Medical Watch," *Globe & Mail*, 27 May 1997, A24. This comes at a time when the Canadian government is considering a single ID card and a central data registry for information sharing among programs—see note 11 to this chapter.

19. Another cost-saving factor already in play that does target individual identities is welfare fraud. Australia uses its tax-file number to compare information from some forty government databases, and claims that this has saved $84 million in its first four years in both administrative costs and fraud. Ijeoma Ross, "Ottawa, Provinces Consider Single ID Card," *Globe & Mail*, 26 May 1997, A1. While Canada, for example, is currently considering a central data registry, the current federal Privacy Act states that personal information gathered for one purpose cannot be used for another, unless for an investigation or the enforcement of any law.

Chapter 3: Information Explosion

1. For a discussion of the difficulties in assessing progress in social science theory, see James B. Rule, *Theory and Progress in Social Science* (Cambridge: Cambridge University Press, 1997).
2. Barry Meier, "Politics of Youth Smoking Fueled by Unproven Data," *New York Times*, 20 May 1998, A1.
3. *The American College Teacher: National Norms for the 1995–96 H.E.R.I. Faculty Survey* (Los Angeles, Calif.: University of California at Los Angeles Higher Education Research Institute, 1997). One justification occasionally offered for this level of scholarly activity is that it enhances the quality of teaching in these institutions. However, John Hattie and H. W. Marsh, in a metastudy of 58 studies, discovered no relationship between the level of scholarship and the quality of teaching. Hattie and Marsh, "The Relationship Between Research and Teaching: A Meta-Analysis," *Review of Educational Research* 66, no. 4 (1996): 507–542.
4. *The 1996 Survey of Earned Doctorates* (Washington, D.C.: National Academy Press, 1997).
5. Burton Bledstein, *The Culture of Professionalism: The Middle Class and the Development of Higher Education in America* (New York: Norton, 1976), 277, 280. Some years ago, Jacques Barzun was already warning that "valuing knowledge, we preposterize the idea . . . [by insisting] everybody shall produce written research in order to live, and it shall be decreed a knowledge explosion." Barzun, *The American University* (New York: Harper and Row, 1968), 221. Graduate student Jeremy Cook recently described the challenge he faced in AIDS research. He began with 23,000 articles published on the topic since 1992; he was able to reduce the number to two thousand by focusing on the two proteins he is studying, and then down to 361 by restricting those to studies on antibodies. See "Overload in the Laboratory: How Much Science Is Too Much Science?" *Globe & Mail*, 29 June 1997, D8.

6. A. M. Cummings et al., *University Libraries and Scholarly Communication: A Study Prepared for the Andrew W. Mellon Foundation* (Washington, D.C.: Association of Research Libraries, 1992), http://www.lib.virginia.edu/mellon/mellon.html; K. E. Marks et al., "Longitudinal Study of Scientific Journal Prices in a Research Library," *College and Research Libraries* 52, no. 2 (1991).

7. M. Johnson and D. Watt, "A Reexamination of Views of Scholarly Publishing and Other Expectations of Productivity in Light of Federal Government Support," in *The Politics and Processes of Scholarship*, ed. J. Moxley and L. T. Lenker (Westport, Conn.: Greenwood Press, 1995), 42.

8. For the loss of consensus and the resulting fragmentation around different forms of history, including women's history, black history, and social history, see Peter Novick, *That Noble Dream: The "Objectivity Question" and the American Historical Profession* (Cambridge: Cambridge University Press, 1988). On the contribution of the social sciences to that loss, see Patrick Manning, "History in the Era of Theory, Methodology, and Multiculturalism," in *Gateways to Knowledge: The Role of Academic Libraries in Teaching, Learning, and Research*, ed. Lawrence Dowler (Cambridge, Mass.: MIT Press, 1997).

9. Bruce A. Bassett and Fabrizio Tamburini, "Inflationary Reheating in Grand Unified Theories," January 1998, http://www.sissa.it/bassett/reheat/.

10. Katie Hafner, "Physics on the Web is Putting Science Journals on the Line," *New York Times*, 21 April 1998, B12.

11. Paul Ginsparg, "First Steps Toward Electronic Research Communication," in *Gateways to Knowledge: The Role of Academic Libraries in Teaching, Learning, and Research*, ed. Lawrence Dowler (Cambridge, Mass.: MIT Press, 1997). The E-print site is at http://xxx.lanl.gov/. Also see Steven Harnad, "The Postgutenberg Galaxy: How to Get There from Here," *The Information Society* 11, no. 4 (1995): 285–91; and http://www.ics.uci.edu/kling/tis.html/.

12. Ibid., "First Steps," 52.

13. Hafner, "Physics," B12.

14. "In an On-Line Salon, Scientists Sit Back and Ponder," *New York Times*, 30 December 1997, B16.

15. Ralph Norman, "The Scholarly Journal and the Intellectual Sensorium," in *The Politics and Processes of Scholarship*, ed. J. Moxley and L. T. Lenker (Westport, Conn.: Greenwood Press, 1995), 80.

16. John Horgan, *The End of Science: Facing The Limits of Knowledge in the Twilight of the Scientific Age* (Reading, Mass.: Addison-Wesley, 1996), 158.

17. David Shenk, *Data Smog: Surviving the Information Glut* (San Francisco,

Calif.: HarperEdge, 1997), 15: "When it comes to information it turns out that you can have too much of a good thing. At a certain level of input, the law of diminishing returns takes effect; the glut of information no longer adds to our quality of life, but instead begins to cultivate stress, confusion, and even ignorance. Information overload threatens our ability to educate ourselves, and leaves us more vulnerable as consumers and less cohesive as a society."

18. Mary Midgely, *Wisdom, Information, and Wonder: What Is Knowledge For?* (London: Routledge, 1994), 7.

19. Diane August and Kenji Hakuta, eds., The Committee on Developing a Research Agenda on the Education of Limited-English-Proficient and Bilingual Students, *Improving Schooling for Language Minority Children: A Research Agenda* (Washington, D.C.: National Academy of Education, 1997), 17.

20. "A Cramped Approach to Bilingualism," *New York Times*, 28 April 1998, A28; National Association for Bilingual Education, June 1998, http://www.nabe.org/unz/.

21. Frank Burni, "Bilingual Education Battle Splits Santa Barbara," *New York Times*, 27 May 1998, A12.

22. Than Bronner, "Bilingual Education Is Facing Push Toward Abandonment," *New York Times*, 30 May 1998, A16.

23. Diane Ravitch, "First Teach Them English," *New York Times*, 5 September 1997, A21.

24. In a recent review of the "education dissemination system," Susan Klein, of the U. S. Department of Education and Margaret K. Gwaltney of COSMOS Corporation call for us to "redesign and manage a national dissemination system" that builds on existing systems including the sixteen clearinghouses (of 100 in the United States) run by ERIC. They point out that earlier initiatives from the 1970s floundered. Klein and Gwaltney, "Charting the Education Dissemination System," *Knowledge: Creation, Diffusion, Utilization* 12, no. 3 (March 1991): 256.

25. ERIC, September 1997, http://ericir.syr.edu/Search/.

26. Jeanne Rennie, of the ERIC Clearinghouse on Languages and Linguistics, reviews research on a variety of models for bilingual education, out of which she has identified factors that are characteristic of effective programs, including parental involvement, training of all teachers in the school, and focusing on functional communication. "ESL and Bilingual Education Programs," ERIC, September 1993, http://www.cal.org/ericcll/digest/Rennie01.htm. Stephen Krashen, "Why Bilingual Education?" ERIC Digest, September 1997, http://www.ed.gov/databases/ERIC Di-

gests/ed403101.html. August and Hakuta (*Improving Schooling*, 318, 316) note the failure of the "research infrastructure" to produce "high quality and relevant research," with widespread dissatisfaction among practitioners and researchers over ignored reports and lack of synthesis. The research is generally marked by "insufficient and incompetent inclusion of language variables in surveys" reflecting a "need for collaboration and coordination" (322–325).

27. National Clearinghouse for Bilingual Education, April 1998, http://www.ncbe.gwu.edu/about.html. Its strength is its reports on exemplary practices and instructional supports rather than bringing order to the vast array of research.

28. G. K. Tallmadge, T. C. M. Lam, and M. L. Camarena report that 98 percent of the 175 studies they examined had several critical design weaknesses. Tallmadge, Lam, and Camarena, *The Evaluation of Bilingual Education Programs for Language Minority, Limited-English-Proficiency Students: A Status Report with Recommendations for Future Developments*, SRA Report 285 (Washington, D.C.: U.S. Department of Education, 1985). Ten years later, Christine Rossell and Keith Baker rejected 75 percent of the 300 program evaluations they examined, with the remaining 72 studies favoring structured immersion in English over transitional bilingual education. "The Educational Effectiveness of Bilingual Education," *Research in the Teaching of English* 30, no. 1 (February 1996): 7–74. To gain some sense of the human story that is lost through the dismissal of ethnographic evaluations, see the wrenching report of Lourdes Diaz Soto in *Language, Culture, and Power: Bilingual Families and the Struggle for Quality Education* (Albany, N.Y.: State University of New York Press, 1997).

29. For example, Peter Behuniak et al. have developed a design for Connecticut that they build into a model for setting national goals, in "Bilingual Education: Evaluation Politics and Practices," *Evaluation Review* 12, no. 5 (October 1988). For a review of federal initiatives in supporting evaluation systems, see Tony C. M. Lam, "Review of Practices and Problems in the Evaluation of Bilingual Education," *Review of Educational Research* 62, no. 2 (summer 1992). An expert panel that reviewed the federally financed $3 million *National Longitudinal Study of the Evaluation of the Effectiveness of Services for Language Minority Limited-English-Proficient Students* and *The Longitudinal Study of Immersion Strategy, Early Exit and Late-Exit Transitional Bilingual Education Programs for Language Minority Children* found that these studies from the 1980s were too flawed to produce useful data. Michael Meyer and Stephen Fine, eds., *The Case of Bilingual Education Strategies* (Washington, D.C.: National Academy Press), 1992.

30. Frederick Shaw, "Bilingual Education: An Idea Whose Time Has Come," *New York Affairs* 3, no. 1 (1975): 108.

31. Gary A. Cziko, "The Evaluation of Bilingual Education: From Necessity and Probability to Possibility," *Educational Researcher* (March 1992): 10.

32. For annual federal and private funding on bilingual education, see the appendix to August and Hakuta, *Improving Schooling*.

33. Bronner, "Bilingual Education," A6.

34. Clifford Geertz, "Learning with Bruner," *New York Review of Books* 44, no. 6 (1997): 22.

35. For the fragmentation in political science, "with members sitting at 'separate tables,'" see Rogers Smith, "Still Blowing in the Wind: The American Quest for a Democratic, Scientific Political Science," *Daedalus* 126, no. 1 (winter 1997): 269. This perception of disciplinary chaos is not exclusive to the human sciences. Humanities professor Marjorie Perloff writes of a public "fed up with the 'contentless' curriculum of literature programs. People have a strong sense that these programs don't teach a particular or coherent body of knowledge and hence are expendable," to which she concedes that "there is surely something to this criticism." Her solution is to shift the emphasis from knowledge to skill by requiring the study of rhetoric as "cultural capital" that pays dividends in law and other disciplines. Perloff, "A Passion for Content: Restoring Literary Literacy to the English Curriculum," *Chronicle of Higher Education* 43, no. 35 (9 May 1997): B4–B5.

36. Ibid.

37. Comte borrowed the metaphor line from Georges Cuvier; Auguste Comte, *Introduction to Positive Philosophy*, trans. Frederick Ferré (Indianapolis, Ind.: Hackett, 1988), 22.

38. Geertz, "Bruner," 22.

39. Jerome Bruner, *The Culture of Education* (Cambridge: Harvard University Press, 1998).

40. Cited by Geertz, "Bruner," 22.

41. Thomas Sowell, *Knowledge and Decisions* (New York: Basic Books, 1980), 26.

42. D. L. Eckberg and L. Hill Jr., "The Paradigm Concept and Sociology: A Critical Review," *American Sociological Review* 44 (1979): 925.

43. Richard Lewontin, "Letter," *New York Review of Books* 44, no. 4 (1997): 52. Also see Burton Bledstein, *The Culture of Professionalism: The Middle Class and the Development of Higher Education in America* (New York: Norton, 1976), 328: "Successful careers depended upon the continual application of scientific thoroughness to limited, specific tasks at specific stages in the course of an occupational lifetime."

Chapter 4: Reading Exasperation

1. Stephen Strauss, "Phonics Reading Methods Best, Study Finds," *Globe & Mail*, 18 February 1997, A1, A7.
2. John Willinsky, "As Some Children Write More than Others: The Impact of Learning to Write," *Alberta Journal of Educational Research* 33 (1987).
3. Strauss, "Phonics," A7.
4. David Booth et al., "Do Children Understand What They Read?" *Globe & Mail*, 3 March 1997, A21.
5. Karin L. Dahl and Penny A. Freppon, "A Comparison of Innercity Children's Interpretation of Reading and Writing Instruction in the Early Grades in Skills-Based and Whole Language Classrooms," *Reading Research Quarterly* 30, no. 1 (January 1995). Although whole-language students "generated significantly more syntactic and lexical features of story language and they experienced extended exposure to and interaction with storybooks" compared to the phonics students, Dahl and Freppon conclude that "the results presented somewhat of a paradoxical picture," largely because of discrepancies between qualitative and quantitative results (70). In another recent instance, H. Sacks and John R. Mergendoller established that in the eleven kindergarten classes they studied, students entering with little knowledge of reading did better, and were more actively engaged in literacy activities, in whole-language-oriented programs on the *Test of Early Reading Ability-2*. Sacks and Mergendoller designed their study to address the lack of studies comparing the two methods using standard measures and large numbers, and they are duly cautious about its impact with better prepared students and in later grades. "The Relationship Between Teachers' Theoretical Orientation Toward Reading and Student Outcomes in Kindergarten with Different Initial Reading Abilities," *American Educational Research Journal* 34, no. 4 (winter 1997).
6. Jacques Steinberg, "Clashing Over Education's One True Faith," *New York Times*, 14 December 1997, WK2, WK14.
7. Ibid.
8. "Hooked on Phonics," *Globe & Mail*, 25 February 1997, A20.
9. Those in government are often prepared, in turn, to claim that useful information is simply not available. Assistant Secretary of the U.S. Department of Education (and member of the scholarly community) Chester Finn once stated that, "to put it simply, our labors [as educational researchers] haven't produced enough findings that Americans use or even see the use of." See C. E. Finn Jr., "What Ails Educational Research," in *Knowledge for Policy: Improving Education Through Research*, ed. D. S. Anderson and B. J. Biddle (London: Falmer, 1991), 39–42.

10. The phonics superiority on the sight-word test is not nearly so great on the U.S. norms scores reported.

11. Bob Udall, *Letting Loose the Hounds* (New York: Norton, 1997) .

12. See my *The New Literacy: Redefining Reading and Writing in the Schools* (New York: Routledge, 1990).

13. Committee on the Prevention of Reading Difficulties in Young Children, *Preventing Reading Difficulties in Young Children* (Washington, D.C.: National Academy Press, 1988), 1–2.

14. Ibid., 18.

15. Jacques Steinberg, "Experts Call for Mix of 2 Methods To Teach Reading," *New York Times*, 19 March 1998, A1, A15.

16. Committee, *Prevention*, 7–8.

17. Steinberg, "Mix," A15.

18. Rebecca Barr et al., eds., *Handbook of Reading Research*, 2 vols. (New York: Longman, 1984, 1991). See also James Flood et al., eds., *Handbook of Research on Teaching the English Language Arts* (New York: Macmillan, 1991), which also includes research on reading and three short references to whole language.

19. Keith E. Stanovich, "Word Recognition: Changing Perspectives," in *Handbook of Reading Research*, ed. Rebecca Barr et al., 2 vols. (New York: Longman, 1984, 1991), 443–44.

20. Ibid.

21. P. David Pearson and Linda Fielding, "Comprehension Instruction," in *Handbook of Reading Research*, ed. Rebecca Barr et al., 2 vols. (New York: Longman, 1984, 1991). Laura R. Roehler and Gerald G. Duffy, "Teacher Instructional Actions," in *Handbook of Reading Research*, ed. Rebecca Barr et al., 2 vols. (New York: Longman, 1984, 1991).

22. Peter Mosenthal and Michael Kamil, "Epilogue," in *Handbook of Reading Research*, ed. Rebecca Barr et al., 2 vols. (New York: Longman, 1984, 1991), 1042.

23. P. G. Aaron, "The Impending Demise of the Discrepancy Formula," *Review of Educational Research* 67, no. 4 (winter 1997).

24. Ibid., 474.

25. Ibid., 476.

Chapter 5: Social Contract

1. Speaking on behalf of the sciences, David H. Guston and Kenneth Keniston identify "a palpable malaise" that has "overtaken the relationship between government and science." See *The Fragile Contract: University Science and the Federal Government* (Cambridge, Mass.: MIT Press), 118.

2. Charles J. Sykes, *Profscam: Professors and the Demise of Higher Education* (New York: St. Martin's, 1990); Roger Kimball, *Tenured Radicals* (New York: Harper & Row, 1990).

3. Among those who would challenge awarding the social sciences this distinction, because of how it seems to exempt the other sciences from this political responsibility, is Joseph Rouse, *Knowledge and Power: Toward a Political Philosophy of Science* (Ithaca, N.Y.: Cornell University Press, 1987), esp. chapter 6.

4. Jean-Jacques Rousseau, *The Social Contract*, trans. G. D. H. Cole (Buffalo, N.Y.: Prometheus Books, 1988), introduction to Book 1. Zoologist Jane Lubchecon, while serving as President of the American Association of the Advancement of Science, proposed a "social contract" in which "scientists will (i) address the urgent needs of society, in proportion to their importance; (ii) communicate their knowledge and understanding widely in order to inform decisions of individuals and institutions; and (iii) exercise good judgment, wisdom, and humility." See "Entering the Century of the Environment: A New Social Contract for Science," *Science* 279 (January 23, 1998): 495.

5. Henri Saint-Simon, "Physiology Applied to the Improvement of Social Institutions: Supplementary Notes," in *Selected Writings on Science, Industry and Social Organization*, trans. Keith Taylor (New York: Holmes & Meier, 1975), 275.

6. Daniel Lerner, "Social Science: Whence and Whither," in *The Human Meaning of the Social Sciences*, ed. Daniel Lerner (New York: Meridian, 1959), 29; Charles Lemert, *Sociology, After the Crisis* (Boulder, Colo.: Westview Press, 1995), ix. While Lerner is brimming with confidence over the impact of social research on social change, Lemert's reassertion of faith is set in the context of a sociology that "has lost its way in the public imagination not simply because of the collapse of the welfare state, which bankrolled the profession's golden age, but because the crisis [of Western domination] was so severe that it caught the profession unawares" (206). The side to the social sciences that is not about being helpful often follows from a philosophical orientation rather than the scientific interests in the field, perhaps most notably with Peter Winch, who in *The Idea of a Social Science* (London: Routledge, 1958) holds that our business is about identifying the spoken and unspoken rules that give meaning to behavior within a culture.

7. Auguste Comte, *The Essential Comte*, trans. Margaret Clarke (New York: Barnes and Noble, 1974), 210.

8. Auguste Comte, *Introduction to Positive Philosophy*, trans. Frederick Ferré (Indianapolis, Ind.: Hackett), 14, 18.

9. Cited in Thomas Haskell, *The Emergence of Professional Social Science: The American Social Science Association and the Nineteenth-Century Crisis of Authority* (Urbana: University of Illinois Press), 101.

10. As political scientist Donald Freeman put it,, there are "no professional value conflicts between a scientific orientation and sophisticated education for democratic citizenship." Freeman, "The Making of a Discipline," in *The Theory and Practice of Political Science*, vol. 1, ed. William Crotty (Evanston, Ill.: Northwestern University Press, 1991), 29. On the political ineffectiveness of the ASSA, compared to the U.K.'s National Association for the Advancement of the Social Sciences, because the American version was made up of professionals, humanitarians and paternalist businessmen, rather than British version of politicians, civil servants and intellectuals, see Libby Schweber, "Progressive Reformers, Unemployment, and the Transformation of Social Inquiry in Britain and the United States, 1880s–1920s," in *States, Social Knowledge, and the Origins of Modern Social Policies*, ed. Dietrich Rueschemeyer and Theda Skocpol (Princeton, N.J.: Princeton University Press, 1996), 181–185.

11. Kenneth Prewitt, "History of SSRC," December 1997, http://www.ssrc.org/histbri.htm. For the argument that sociology, at least, could only have achieved "coherence and diffusion" through university departmentalization, see Edward Shils, "The Place of Sociology," in *The Calling of Sociology and Other Essays on the Pursuit of Learning* (Chicago: University of Chicago Press, 1980), 4ff.

12. Robert S. Lynd, *Knowledge for What? The Place of Social Science in American Culture* (Princeton, N.J.: Princeton University Press, 1939).

13. Ibid., 10, 118.

14. Ibid., 129.

15. Ibid., 209.

16. Shils, "Sociology," 71 n. 4: "The term 'applied research' in the social sciences refers to investigations performed for policy-makers who will presumably take the resulting propositions into account in their decisions . . . . It is not applied research in the sense of the application of scientifically tested general principles obtained in 'basic' or 'pure' research to the explanation of concrete and particular situations or the management or construction of concrete and particular constellations of actions."

17. Robert P. Nathan, *Social Science in Government: Uses and Misuses* (New York: Basic Books, 1988), 18, 19. Nathan proposes that if we "change the way we do business" through improved research design and practices, the social sciences can help government "to deal with and resolve social problems." We need to stay focused on "how to do things."

18. For example, Shils ("Sociology," 81) speaks of how it has long been accepted, as part of the "dominant tradition . . . that sociologists should address themselves to a larger audience than the academic world."

19. C. Wright Mills, *The Sociological Imagination* (New York: Oxford University Press, 1959), 100, 101, 117. See also Shils, "Sociology," 37: "Sociology would be a moral monstrosity if, after its decent adolescence, it were in its riper years to develop into a tool for technocrats to rule the human race— presumably for its benefit."

20. William M. Epstein, *Welfare in America: How Social Science Fails the Poor* (Madison: University of Wisconsin Press, 1997).

21. Charles Murray, *Losing Ground: American Social Policy, 1950–1980* (New York: Basic Books, 1984), 198.

22. Epstein, *Welfare in America*, 63. There is also the problem of what Epstein identifies as "the extensive 'fugitive' ephemeral welfare literature," which muddies the results for want of any review process (45 n. 5).

23. Ibid., 4, 26. Following the arguments of Nathan Glazer, Epstein writes: "The limitations exact a price from the social sciences: The absence of true tests of causality creates an opening for bias that drains their authority" (Ibid., 30). See Nathan Glazer, *The Limits of Social Policy* (Cambridge: Harvard University Press, 1988), 1, 6.

24. Robert H. Haveman, one of the key researchers in the War on Poverty, is among those who have used the metaphor of referee, although he also holds that the "rather different ideological perspective and interpretation" was a healthy influence on researchers, countering the rationalist tendencies that drove the War on Poverty. See *Poverty Policy and Poverty Research: The Great Society and the Social Sciences* (Madison: University of Wisconsin Press, 1987), 235–36.

25. Cited by Neal Kumar Katyal, "National Testing's Pedigree," *New York Times*, 12 September 1997, A19.

26. National Science Foundation, May 1998, http://www.nsf.gov/sbe/ sbeovrvw.htm. For a scathing review of the corrupting influence of grant writing on philosophy, with obvious relevance to the social sciences, leading to puffery and groundless claims of social good that inevitably erode intellectual honesty, see Susan Haack, "Preposterism and Its Consequences," in *Scientific Innovation, Philosophy and Public Policy*, ed. Ellen Frankel Paul, Fred D. Miller, Jr., and Jeffrey Paul (Cambridge: Cambridge University Press, 1996).

27. "The Sociology Program supports research on problems of human social organization, demography, and processes of individual and institutional change. The Program encourages theoretically focused empirical investi-

gations aimed at improving the explanation of fundamental social processes. Included is research on organizations and organizational behavior, population dynamics, social movements, social groups, labor force participation, stratification and mobility, family, social networks, socialization, gender roles, and the sociology of science and technology. In assessing the intrinsic merit of a proposed piece of research, four components are key to securing support from the Sociology Program: (1) The issues investigated must be theoretically grounded. (2) The research should be based on empirical observation or be subject to empirical validation. (3) The research design must be appropriate to the questions asked. (4) The proposed research must advance our understanding of social processes or social structures." February 1998, http://www.nsf.gov/sbe/sber/sociol/start.htm.

28. From the NSF web site: "Earthquake Hazards and Residential Location: Risa Palm of the University of Oregon has conducted extensive research on earthquake hazard perception in Southern California. Disclosure of hazards by real estate agents does not effectively convey information about risk to home buyers. Palm's findings have been presented in testimony to California Seismic Safety Commission and the U.S. Congress. Her research results suggest the need for a national earthquake reinsurance program comparable to that in effect for flood insurance." February 1998, http://www.nsf.gov/sbe/sber/features/29.htm. "Balinese Water Temples: For centuries, farmers in the dramatically-stepped wet-rice terraces of Bali relied on priests of local 'water temples' to coordinate irrigation among hundreds of farming communities." February 1998, http://www.nsf.gov/sbe/sber/features/27.htm.

29. Budget figures as of February 1998 are found at http://www.nsf.gov/bfa/start.htm. An additional $611 million is spent on education and human resources development research, which was devoted to improving science, mathematics, engineering, and technology education, and involved social science research in many cases. The federal government also funds research in education to the tune of $123 million in 1997, with an additional $50 million for the National Center for Education Statistics, "in order to promote and accelerate the improvement of American Education," according to its web site (May 1998), http://nces.ed.gov/. For a point of comparison between federal research support for the sciences and the humanities, the National Endowment for the Humanities was allotted $110 million for 1997. Another (admittedly crude) way to look at how much is being invested in social science research is to take the rule of thirds: that a faculty member at a four-year institution should be devoting one-third of his or her time to research, with average salaries for 1996 at $50,000. The roughly

170,000 faculty involved in the social sciences, devoting a third of their time to research, would amount to an investment by students, benefactors, and public funds of $2.8 billion dollars in salaries, on top of which we would have to add the infrastructure costs of support staff, building, etc. Figures drawn from *Chronicle of High Education* http://chronicle.com.

30. Jules Feiffer, "Op-Art," *New York Times*, 17 October 1997, A19.

31. Chava Frankfort-Nachmias and David Nachmias, *Research Methods in the Social Sciences*, 5th ed. (New York: St. Martin's Press, 1996).

32. Ibid., 66. For a description of the U.K.'s Social Science Research Council's (SSRC) Open Door program, in which "client users" (including unions, managers, and professionals), in collaboration with social scientists, initiated and defined SSRC-funded research projects, see John Gill, "Research as Action: Experiment in Utilizing the Social Sciences," in *The Use and Abuse of Social Science*, ed. Frank Heller (London: Sage, 1986).

33. Frankfurt-Nachmias and Nachmias's book includes an appendix by Nina Reshef with additional advice on choosing a topic. Reshef recommends, among other things, that researchers "[a]void topics that have been extensively researched." Frankfurt-Nachmias and Nachmias, *Research Methods*, 558.

34. Richard M. Lerner and Lou Anna K. Simon, *University-Community Collaborations for the Twenty-first Century: Outreach Scholarship for Youth and Families* (New York: Garland, 1998).

35. Rogers Smith, "Still Blowing in the Wind: The American Quest for a Democratic, Scientific Political Science," *Daedalus* 126, no. 1 (winter 1997): 276–77.

36. Ibid., 254.

37. Ibid., 257, emphasis in original.

38. Frankfurt-Nachmias and Nachmias, *Research Methods*, 77.

39. Ibid., 91–95.

40. Gary T. Marx, "Of Methods and Manners for Aspiring Sociologists: 37 Moral Imperatives," *American Sociologist* 8, no. 1 (1997): 102–125.

41. Ibid., 103.

42. Ibid., 122.

43. Ibid., 123–24. Cf. Maureen Hallinan, "A Sociological Perspective on Social Issues," *American Sociologist* 28, no. 1 (1997): 11. Hallinan holds that sociology falls short of developing "powerful theory" due to "a lack of faith in the power of the discipline and a weakness of will to take on the task."

44. As president of the American Sociological Association, Maureen Hallinan ("Sociological Perspective") compared sociologist James Coleman to Charles Dickens. On the complexity of life compared to airplanes, a recent

report points out that at Boeing "engineers spend 50,000 to 380,000 hours —at a cost of $7.5 million to $57 million dollars—simply specifying which of as many as six million parts go into each plane." See Lawrence Zuckerman, "Stacked Up at Boeing," *New York Times*, 14 November 1997, C4.

45. Diane August and Kenji Hakuta, eds., *Improving Schooling for Language Minority Children: A Research Agenda* (Washington, D.C.: National Academy of Education, 1997), 317.

46. On science's social contract and peer review, Guston and Keniston write: "The bargain struck between the federal government and university science—what we call the 'social contract for science'—can be summarized in a few words: Government promises to fund the basic science that peer reviewers find most worthy of support, and scientists promise that the research will be performed well and honestly and will provide a steady stream of discoveries that can be translated into new products, medicines, or weapons." Guston and Keniston, *Fragile Contract*, 1–2.

47. Herbert London, "Resisting Frivolity in Academe," *Chronicle of Higher Education*, 22 May 1998, B7.

48. Cited by Thomas Haskell, "Justifying the Rights of Academic Freedom in the Era of 'Power/Knowledge,'" in *The Future of Academic Freedom*, ed. Louis Menand (Chicago: University of Chicago Press, 1996), 57–58.

49. Richard Rorty, "Does Academic Freedom Have Philosophical Presuppositions?" in *The Future of Academic Freedom*, ed. Louis Menand (Chicago: University of Chicago Press, 1996), 20.

50. Ibid., 28.

51. Ibid., 27.

52. Ibid., 34. Rorty is citing from Dewey's *The Quest for Certainty*. Dewey's position was challenged, it is worth noting, by Thorstein Veblen, who held that science, and no less social science, accrued from "idle curiosity." Veblen countered his own theory of the leisured (academic) class with a technocratic faith in society's ability to eliminate inefficiencies and waste; see Dorothy Ross, "Social Science and the Idea of Progress," in *The Authority of Experts: Studies in History and Theory*, ed. Thomas L. Haskell (Bloomington: Indiana University Press, 1984), 165–185.

53. The handiness of sport's statistical obsession when it comes to the social sciences comes up in Jackie Robinson's career as the first African American major-league baseball player. Proof of the prejudice he initially faced in the league comes in the form of the six times he was hit by pitchers in his first 37 games, which was the most anyone had been hit during the entire National League season the year before. That he was only hit three more times during the rest of the season provides some insight into how his courage at

the plate came to be respected. See *Arnold Rampersad, Jackie Robinson: A Biography* (New York: Knopf, 1997).

54. *New York Times*, 24 October 1997, C3.

Chapter 6: Technologies of Knowledge

1. David Zeitlyn, *The Virtual Institute of Mambila Studies*, May 1997, http://lucy.ukc.ac.uk/dz/.
2. Lawrence K. Altman, "British Cast Spotlight on Misconduct in Scientific Research," *New York Times*, 9 June 1998, D8.
3. Ricki Goldman-Segall, *Points of Viewing Children's Thinking: A Digital Ethnographer's Journey* (New York: Lawrence Erlbaum, 1998).
4. Christopher Shea, "Taking Aim at the 'Ken Burns' View of the Civil War," *Chronicle of Higher Education*, 20 March 1998, A16–A17. Edward Ayer's "Valley of the Shadow" is, as of May 1998, at http://jefferson.village.virginia.edu/vshadow2/.
5. Another book-support project that places a somewhat different data set on the web is the *Cigarette Papers Online*, mounted by the Center for Knowledge Management at the University of California at San Francisco. It includes the documents, many of them anonymously donated to the university, accompanying the tobacco company's research on smoking, as well as the Brown & Williamson search for a safer cigarette. Center for Knowledge Management at the University of California, San Francisco, April 1998, http://www.ckm.ucsf.edu/projects.
6. Richard Rockwell, "Using Electronic Social Science Data in the Age of the Internet," in *Gateways to Knowledge: The Role of Academic Libraries in Teaching, Learning, and Research*, ed. Lawrence Dowler (Cambridge, Mass.: MIT Press, 1997).
7. Ibid., 69–70.
8. See David Friedman, "A World of Strong Privacy," in *Scientific Innovation, Philosophy and Public Policy*, ed. Ellen Frankel Paul, Fred D. Miller, Jr., and Jeffrey Paul (Cambridge: Cambridge University Press, 1996); John Markoff, "Guidelines Don't End Debate on Internet Privacy," *New York Times*, 18 December 1998, A21. See also Edmund F. Byrne, "The Two-Tiered Ethics of Electronic Data Processing," *Philosophy of Technology*, April 1998, http://scholar.lib.vt.edu/ejournals/SPT/v2_n1html/byrne.html/
9. K. Krechmer, "Recommendations for the Global Information Highway: A Matter of Standards," *Information Standards Quarterly* 8, no. 1 (1996): 1–5.
10. M. H. Needleman, "Standards for the Global Information Infrastructure," *Information Standards Quarterly* 8, no. 2 (1996): 1–5.
11. The Government Information Locator System (GILS) is a U.S. federal

standard under consideration by other governments. Another protocol has been developed for automating interlibrary loans, with developments underway for museums, serials, and other types of digital collections. With databases, a global standard is emerging with SQL (Structured Query Language), a tool for searching relational databases that has been adopted by the major database vendors. An international "information system for the management of agricultural research" covers national agricultural research programs. By 1996 twelve nations were contributing to this database, which covers people, finances, resources, experiments, and research reports. See D. Vernon, "INFORM: An Information System for the Management of Agricultural Research," *Information Development* 11, no. 1 (1996): 31–35.

12. Jean-Claude Guédon, "Electronic Academic Journals: From Disciplines to 'Seminars,'" in *Computer Networking and Scholarly Communication in the Twenty-First Century*, ed. T. M. Harrison and T. Stephen (Albany: State University of New York Press, 1966), 346.

13. Robert Cameron, "A Universal Citation Database as a Catalyst for Reform in Scholarly Communication," *First Monday* 2, no. 4 (1997), available at http://www.firstmonday.dk/issues/issue2 4/cameron/index.html.

14. That is, Andrew Leonard, *Bots: The Origin of New Species* (New York: Hardwired, 1997), which I had only spotted in a bookstore before I tracked it down at Amazon.com.

15. "Datamine," *Data Mining and Knowledge Discovery: An International Journal*, February 1997, http://www.research.microsoft.com/research/datamine/. Those involved in this field realized they had a new discipline in the making when five hundred people showed up at the Second International Conference on Knowledge Discovery and Data Mining in Oregon in 1996.

16. For the continuing statistical shortcomings data mining faces, see Clark Glymour et al., "Statistical Themes and Lessons for Data Mining," *Data Mining and Knowledge Discovery* 1, no. 1 (1997): 15.

17. I. Bhandari et al., "Advanced Scout: Data Mining and Knowledge Discovery in NBA Data," *Data Mining and Knowledge Discovery* 1, no. 1 (1997); George Johnson, "Undiscovered Bach? No, a Computer Wrote It," *New York Times*, 11 November 1997, B9–B10.

18. Northern Ireland Knowledge Engineering Laboratory, May 1998, http://www.nikel.ulst.ac.uk/.

19. Reported in H. Jack Greiger, "Marked-Down Medicine," *New York Times Book Review*, 21 December 1997, 26, and Enrico Coiera, "Evidence Based Medicine, the Internet, and the Rise of Medical Infomatics," Hewlett Packard Research Laboratories, December 1997, http://www.hpl.hp.com/techreports/96/HPL-96–26.html.

20. David L. Sackett et al., *Evidence-Based Medicine: What It Is and What It*

Isn't (Oxford: Centre for Evidence-Based Medicine, 1997); December 1997, http://cebm.jr2.ox.ac.uk/ebmisisnt.html.

21. That a patient's health may respond to this knowledge may be very tentatively suggested by the proven success of placebos on a range of conditions such as colds, asthma, and heart disease, which, Walter A. Brown proposes, may be due to patients' greater sense of involvement in their treatment and cure. "The Placebo Effect," *Scientific American*, January 1998.

22. Sackett et al., *Evidence-Based Medicine*.

23. For a review of the continuing bias against clinical research, see Paulette Walker Campbell, "What Ails Clinical Research?" *Chronicle of Higher Education*, 23 January 1998, A31–A32. It is worth comparing with Eugene J. Meehan's study of the economics literature, in which he found that more than 90 percent of the research, over a ten-year period, had no relevance for policy, with 90–95 percent dealing with technical problems within the research. Meehan, *Economics and Policymaking: The Tragic Illusion* (Westport, Conn.: Greenwood Press, 1982), 26.

24. Sackett et al., *Evidence-Based Medicine*.

25. Abigail Zuger, "New Way of Doctoring: By the Book," *New York Times*, 16 December 1997, B14.

26. "*ACP Journal Club*'s general purpose is to select from the biomedical literature those articles reporting studies and reviews that warrant immediate attention by physicians attempting to keep pace with important advances in internal medicine. These articles are summarized in 'value added' abstracts and commented on by clinical experts." *ACP Journal Club*, May 1998, http://cebm.jr2.ox.ac.uk/docs/hiru/acpjc/default.htm.

27. Abstract subtitles include Objective, Data Sources, Study Selection, Data Extraction, Main Results, and Conclusion. The Results often include financial calculations for professional care and hospital stays, which when related to mortality rates offer a chilling instance of cost-benefit analyses. Managed-care and health insurance systems are bound to be interested in such mathematics, but Sackett is adamant that this approach could support the use of more expensive tests or treatments as easily as it could justifycheaper methods. Michael Millenson makes the case for the connection between this form of "medical excellence," as he terms it, and for-profit managed-care health systems. Millenson, *Demanding Medical Excellence: Doctors and Accountability in the Information Age* (Chicago: University of Chicago Press, 1997).

28. David Barer, "Commentary," *American College of Physician's Journal Club*, December 1997, http://www.acponline.org/journals/acpjc/novdec97/strokeun.htm.

29. Robert Pear, "Medical Research to Get More Money from Government," *New York Times*, 3 January 1998, A1, A8.

30. With a 1997 budget of $440 million, the National Center for Research Resources operates in association with the National Institutes of Health in Bethesda, Maryland. The Center provides access to state-of-the art shared instrumentation high performance computing, molecular and cellular structural biology technologies, biomedical engineering, noninvasive imaging and spectroscopy, and mathematical modeling and computer simulations. National Center for Research Resources, February 1998, http://www.ncrr.nih.gov/.

31. Zuger, "New Way," B14. Zuger presents outcome analysis as an alternative to EBM, which favors clinical trials, but there is no reason in principle why the evidence drawn from outcome analysis could not serve EBM.

32. Geiger, "Marked-Down Medicine," 24. Taking their cues from the military's expert systems for diagnosing engines and target recognition, hospitals are employing Health Informatics Systems with electronic data capture for patients by using wireless computers integrated into medical consultation networks that include knowledge bases, decision supports, and cost management. The result has proven to be improvements in both cost reduction and assignment of appropriate therapies. Paul Anderson, "Diagnostic and Document Medical Images Meet Decision Support Systems," *Advanced Imaging* 12 (September 1997): 38–42.

33. Zuger, "New Way," B14.

34. Ivan Illich, "Disabling Professions," in *Disabling Professions*, ed. Ivan Illich et al. (London: Marion Boyars, 1977), 18.

35. Ivan Illich, *Tools for Conviviality* (London: Marion Boyars, 1982).

36. Bruce G. Buchanan and Edward H. Shortliffe, eds., *Rule-Based Expert Systems: The MYCIN Experiments of the Stanford Heuristic Programming Project* (Reading, Mass.: Addison-Wesley, 1984). James H. Fetzer, "Computer Reliability and Public Policy: Limits of Knowledge of Computer-Based Systems," in *Scientific Innovation, Philosophy and Public Policy*, ed. Ellen Frankel Paul, Fred D. Miller Jr., and Jeffrey Paul (Cambridge: Cambridge University Press, 1996); Alison Cawsey, *Databases and Artificial Intelligence*, May 1998, http://www.cee.hw.ac.uk/. Clearly, the namers of MYCIN lacked a phonetic sense of irony with regard to their creation of artificial intelligence. The late internal medicine specialist Jack Myers developed a system that matched 3,550 symptoms with more than 500 diseases, only to replace it with Q. M. R., still being sold by First Databank, which scans a database of coded research reports as well as his own diagnostic knowledge, even as he called for a uniform national database to support such work: Ford

Burkhart, "Dr. Jack Meyers, 84, a Pioneer In Computer-Aided Diagnoses," *New York Times*, 22 February 1998, 23.

37. *OncoLink*, May 1998, http://cancer.med.upenn.edu/. How useful has this site proven over its four years? OncoLink includes glowing testimonials from its press coverage, and it offers the figures on the traffic at the site: "OncoLink incurred 44,259,780 transactions from 1,748,214 unique IP addresses between March 7, 1994 and December 31, 1997."

38. Jean-François Lyotard, *The Postmodern Condition: A Report on Knowledge*, trans. G. Bennington and B. Massumi (Minneapolis: University of Minnesota Press, 1984), 4.

39. See Langdon Winner, *Autonomous Technology: Technics-of-Control as Theme in Political Thought* (Cambridge, Mass.: MIT Press, 1978): "The newly emergent vogue of the idea makes it clear that, if nothing, else, 'autonomous technology' has enough intuitive plausibility to stand as a convenient receptacle of a host of contemporary anxieties" (15). There is also Rorty: "Heidegger's neo-Nietzschean conviction that our Baconian, technological culture has reduced our stature—made us moral and spiritual pygmies—is equally implausible." Rorty, "Against Unity," *Wilson Quarterly* (winter 1998): 36.

40. It is worth recalling, if only in a footnote, the 1960s philosopher-hero Herbert Marcuse's insistence that technology "projected what a society and its ruling interests intend to do with men and things," and it may be that we can now use those projections to both identify our place in "the technical apparatus" and jury-rig it to achieve different ends. Herbert Marcuse, "Industrialization and Capitalism in the Work of Max Weber," in *Negations: Essays in Critical Theory*, trans. Jeremy J. Shapiro (Boston: BeaconPress, 1968), 223.

Chapter 7: Enlightenment, Democracy, Knowledge

1. Immanuel Kant, *Was ist Aufklärung*, trans. Lewis White Beck, in Michel Foucault, *The Politics of Truth* (New York: Semiotext[e], 1997).

2. Ibid., 7.

3. See Charles Mills, *The Racial Contract* (Ithaca, N.Y.: Cornell University Press, 1997), 16: "The color-coded morality of the Racial Contract restricts the possession of this [Kantian] natural freedom and equality to white men."

4. Rogers Smith, "Still Blowing in the Wind: The American Quest for a Democratic, Scientific Political Science," *Daedalus* 126, no. 1 (winter 1997): 275–76. Smith cites and supports Charles Lindblom's *Inquiry and Change: The*

Troubled Attempt to Understand and Shape Society (New Haven, Conn.: Yale University Press, 1990).

5. Fyodor Dostoevsky, *Notes from Underground*, trans. Ralph E. Matlaw (New York: Dutton, 1960).

6. Ibid., 28.

7. Ibid., 29, emphasis in original.

8. Ibid., 29.

9. Thomas L. Haskell, "Introduction," in Haskell, ed., *The Authority of Experts: Studies in History and Theory* (Bloomington: Indiana University Press, 1984), x.

10. See Dorothy Ross, "Social Science and the Idea of Progress," in *The Authority of Experts: Studies in History and Theory*, ed. Thomas L. Haskell (Bloomington: Indiana University Press, 1984).

11. Edward Ross, *Social Control* (New York: Macmillan, 1901), 441.

12. B. F. Skinner, *Beyond Freedom and Dignity* (New York: Knopf, 1971), 205.

13. William Bechtel, "Responsibility and Decision Making in the Era of Neural Networks," in *Scientific Innovation, Philosophy and Public Policy*, ed. Ellen Frankel Paul, Fred D. Miller Jr., and Jeffrey Paul (Cambridge: Cambridge University Press, 1996), 294–95.

14. On the power and the expert, see Magali Sarfatti Larson, "The Production of Expertise and Constitution of Expert Power," in *The Authority of Experts: Studies in History and Theory*, ed. Thomas L. Haskell (Bloomington: Indiana University Press, 1984). Neo-Kantian Jürgen Habermas also made the point in addressing the science of public opinion: "The question is rather whether a productive body of knowledge is merely transmitted to men engaged in technical manipulation for purposes of control or is simultaneously appropriated as the linguistic possession of communicating individuals." "The Scientization of Politics and Public Opinion," in *Toward a Rational Society: Student Protest, Science, and Politics*, trans. Jeremy J. Shapiro (Boston: Beacon Press, 1970), 79.

15. Ivan Illich, *The Disabling Professions* (London: Marion Boyars, 1977).

16. Gertrude Himmelfarb, "Revolution in the Library," *American Scholar* 66 (spring 1997): 199–202.

17. Or in Jürgen Habermas's neo-Kantian analysis, is it an instance of "reason that puts itself on trial?" *Between Fact and Norms*, trans. William Rehg, cited in John Rawls, *Political Liberalism* (New York: Columbia University Press, 1996), 377.

18. Alexis de Tocqueville, *Democracy in America*, vol. 2, ed. Phillips Bradley (New York: Vintage Books, 1945), 4–5, 42. Cited by Yaron Ezrahi, "Technology and the Civil Epistemology of Democracy," in *Technology and the Poli-*

tics of Knowledge, ed. Andrew Feenberg and Alastair Hannay (Blooming-ton: Indiana University Press, 1990), 160.

19. Ibid., 160.

20. Ibid., 165. Ezrahi reaches back to the example of the seventeenth-century scientist Robert Boyle, who did much to introduce scientific reasoning to the popular imagination by devising, in Ezrahi's words, "a host of strate-gies and techniques for socially augmenting and diffusing the power of the experimental situation to establish facts among publics that did not actu-ally attend and witness the event."

21. Donna Haraway, "Situated Knowledges: The Science Question in Femi-nism and the Privilege of Partial Perspective," in *Technology and the Politics of Knowledge*, ed. Andrew Feenberg and Alastair Hannay (Bloomington: Indiana University Press, 1990), 185. Haraway argues for "the potent politics and epistemologies of embodied, and therefore, accountable, objectivity." Although Haraway disparages the Enlightenment's universalized rational-ity in favor of ethnophilosophies, she goes on to write, with great relevance for Automata Data, about webbed accounts: "Webs can have the property of being systematic, even of being centrally structured global systems with deep filaments and tenacious tendrils into time, space, and consciousness, which are the dimensions of world history" (Ibid., emphasis in original).

22. On the immaturity of the social sciences, see Paul A. Roth, *Meaning and Method in the Social Sciences: A Case for Methodological Pluralism* (Ithaca, N.Y.: Cornell University Press, 1987). In the terms of a postmodern politics of truth, Automata Data could indeed feed Michel Foucault's great fear of "the never radically contested but still all massive and ever-growing estab-lishment of a vast technical and scientific system." "What Is Critique?" in *The Politics of Truth*, trans. Lysa Hochroth (New York: Semiotext[e], 1997), 43. Automata Data builds on, rather than against, the larger system. Re-writing academic subroutines to strengthen the coherence of research re-sults leads to a more robust technical system of refined and effective knowl-edge production. Yet I would also hold that Automata Data stands with Foucault "against the claims of a unitary body of theory which would filter, heirarchise and order . . . in the name of some true knowledge and some arbitrary idea of what constitutes a science and its objects." Automata Data would undermine the unity and singularity of a true knowledge, while making the diversity of knowing available to people, not least of all in their struggle against the vast technical and scientific system. "Two Lectures," in *Power/Knowledge: Selected Interviews and Other Writings 1972–1977*, trans. by Alessandro Fontana and Pasquale Pasquino (New York: Pantheon, 1980), 83.

23. We might then have to acknowledge that, as the Frankfurt School philosopher Theodor Adorno insisted, rather than changing the world, what the intellectual really wants is only to be at some point read exactly as intended. See Edward Said, *Representations of the Intellectual* (New York: Vintage, 1996), 42.

24. Richard Herrnstein and Charles Murray, *The Bell Curve: Intelligence and Class Structure in American Life* (New York: Free Press, 1994).

25. Harvard biologist Stephen Jay Gould, himself a best seller among science writers, expresses his suspicions of a book that "garners as much attention as The Bell Curve." He puts the book's popularity down to the distemper of the times. "Curveball," in *The Bell Curve Wars: Race, Intelligence, and the Future of America*, ed. Stephen Fraser (New York: Basic Books, 1995), 11. Similarly, another Harvard man, Howard Gardner, begins his critique by noting how the book has been labeled "as a 'big,' 'important,' and 'controversial' book," again suggesting something is clearly inverted in this instance besides the contemptuous commas." "Cracking Open the IQ Box," in *The Bell Curve Wars: Race, Intelligence, and the Future of America*, ed. Stephen Fraser (New York: Basic Books, 1995), 23. For me at least, this popularity or sense of importance cannot be the complaint. It is surely nothing more than these gentleman seek through their own prolific flow of books.

26. Herrnstein and Murray, *Bell Curve*, 6–7.

27. Stephen Jay Gould, *The Mismeasure of Man* (New York: Norton, 1981).

28. Herrnstein and Murray, *Bell Curve*, 311. "We are resolutely agnostic on that issue; as far as we can determine, the evidence does not yet justify an estimate" of genetic influence on IQ by race.

29. Ibid., 520. Also: "Until the latter half of this century, it was taken for granted that one of the chief purposes of education was to educate the gifted . . . . Little will change until educators once again embrace this aspect of their vocation" (Ibid., 418).

30. Ibid., 4. Given that I suggested earlier that in this fantasy the Board of Directors for Automata Data would include Nobel Prize winners, I had better allow for another William Shockley, a Nobel Prize winning physicist, who was among those advocating, a generation ago, eugenic policies based on IQ.

31. Gould, *Mismeasure*, 17.

32. Ulric Neisser, ed., *The Rising Curve: Long-Term Gains in IQ and Related Measures* (Washington, D.C.: American Psychological Association, 1988).

33. Richard Nisbett, "Race, IQ, and Scientism," in *The Bell Curve Wars: Race, Intelligence, and the Future of America*, ed. Stephen Fraser (New York: Basic Books, 1995), 53.

34. Nathan Glazer wrote *Affirmative Discrimination: Ethnic Inequality and Public Policy* (New York: Basic Books, 1975) in 1975, and *We Are All Multiculturalists Now* (Cambridge: Harvard University Press, 1997) two decades later, attributing the changes of heart between the two books to the failure of integration in America.
35. The distinguished sociologist James S. Coleman, at the University of Chicago, notes that there have been proposals for "science courts" for deciding controversies, while the more interesting proposal idea he reports on is "that two or more research projects be carried out on the same topic, guided by differing interests." He also reminds us that "policy research pluralistically formulated and openly published may strengthen the hand of those interests without administrative authority, by redressing the imbalance between those in authority and those outside." "The Structure of Society and the Nature of Social Science Research," *Knowledge: Creation, Diffusion, Utilization* 1 (1980): 347.
36. Thomas Sowell, *The Vision of the Anointed: Self-Congratulation as a Basis for Social Policy* (New York: Basic Books, 1995), 2.
37. Ibid., 64, 143.
38. *The Wall Street Journal* back-cover blurb seems particularly ironic in calling the book "as compelling an explanation as any for the seemingly disproportionate amount of condescension and politically correct invective that emanates from the liberal side of the political spectrum toward the conservative opposition."
39. Sowell, *Anointed*, 12.
40. Alan Wolfe, "Scholarship on Family Values: Weighing Competing Claims," *Chronicle of Higher Education*, 23 January 1998, B8; Jessie Bernard, *The Future of Marriage* (New Haven, Conn.: Yale University Press, 1973); Arlene Skolnick, *The Intimate Environment* (New York: HarperCollins; 1996); Stephanie Coontz, *The Way We Never Were* (New York: Basic Books, 1992).
41. Eric Eckholm, "China Cracks Down on Dissent in Cyberspace," *New York Times*, 31 December 1997, A3.
42. Howard Rheingold, *The Virtual Community* (Reading, Mass.: Addison-Wesley, 1993), 14.
43. Ibid., 285.
44. One effect of the rise of academic professions such as the social sciences, historian Thomas Bender has argued, is a specialization of expertise and language that has resulted in "an impoverished public culture [with] little means for critical discussion of general ideas." That may be overstated, judging from the undiminished newsstands, not to mention the burgeoning public culture of the Internet, but Bender's concern over how intellectual expertise can become divorced from intellectual public culture is

clearly a concern of mine as well. Thomas Bender, "The Erosion of Public Culture: Cities, Discourses, and Professional Disciplines," in *The Authority of Experts: Studies in History and Theory*, ed. Thomas L. Haskell (Bloomington: Indiana University Press, 1984), 101.

45. Richard E. Sclove, *Democracy and Technology* (New York: Guilford Press), 50, 53.

Chapter 8: Knowledge Futures

1. Deborah Shapely, "The da Vinci of Data," *New York Times*, 30 March 1998, C8.

2. Robert Coles, "Editor's Story," *DoubleTake* 12 (spring 1988): 4.

3. Edward Shils, "The Place of Sociology," in *The Calling of Sociology and Other Essays on the Pursuit of Learning* (Chicago: University of Chicago Press, 1980), 92.

4. See John Willinsky and Shannon Bradley Green, "Desktop Publishing in Remedial Language Arts Settings: Letting Them Eat Cake," *Journal of Teaching Writing* 9 no. 2 (1991), and my "Tempering the Masculinities of Technology," in *Masculinity in the High School*, ed. Nancy Lesko (Thousand Oaks, Calif.: Sage, in press).

5. See my "When University Students Word Process Their Assignments," *Computers in the Schools* 6, no. l/2 (1989).

6. Todd Oppenheimer, "The Computer Delusion," *Atlantic Monthly*, July 1997, 45–62; http://www.theatlantic.com/issues/97jul/computer.htm.

7. Ibid., 47.

8. Andrew Trotter, "Taking Technology's Measure," *Education Week*, 10 November 1997, 11.

9. Neil J. Smelser, *Problematics of Sociology* (Berkeley: University of California Press, 1997).

10. Pablo González Casanova, *The Fallacy of Social Science Research: A Critical Examination and New Qualitative Model* (New York: Pergamon, 1981).

11. Immanuel Wallerstein, *The Modern World-System*, vols. 1–3 (New York: Academic Press, 1974–1978). Smelser (*Sociology*, 89) speaks of the formation of a new "service proletariat" that needs to be observed on a global scale, as well as a hope that "the internationalization of social problems and the accompanying realization that they are world systematic in character will, it is hoped, provide a major impulse for legal and other forms of international intervention."

12. Martha Nussbaum, "Through the Prism of Gender," *Times Literary Supplement*, 20 March 1998, 3.

13. On the relative failure of the social science efforts of UNESCO, see Peter

Lengyel, "Misapplication of Social Science at UNESCO," in *The Use and Abuse of Social Science*, ed. Frank Heller (London: Sage, 1986). Dating back to 1946, UNESCO had a social science division, amid concerns about the disciplines' cultural biases and the need for indigenization. Lengyel blames the social sciences as a whole: "The profession has been notably negligent and incoherent in grasping the opportunities opened up by access to the unique international base at UNESCO" (59).

14. The parallel with military intelligence bears considering, with a group of a dozen scientists, known as Medea, recently given access to the massive geopolitical data gathered during the Cold War at a cost of several hundred billions of dollars: "The notion being that much of this information gathered for intelligence or military purposes is scientifically useful and that, moreover, it can be put to scientific use without compromising any of the intelligence or military imperatives—such as secrecy—under which it was originally collected and used." Jeffrey T. Richelson, "Scientists in Black," *Scientific American*, February 1998, 48. Among commercial data sources, Metromail Corp. has information on 103 million people (it sells access at 25 cents a name), representing 95 percent of American households, while Britain's Great Universal Stores, which has been trying to acquire Metromail, has information on 780 million people in seventeen countries. Robert Berner and Ernest Beck, "Metromail's Data Are the Spoils of Takeover War," *Wall Street Journal*, 30 March 1998, B1.

15. The difficulty in estimating such figures is based on category problems. The U.S. government's funding of research in almost all of its categories, including Defense, Health and Human Services, and National Science Foundation, include many social science components. The federal fiscal estimate for 1998 includes $189 million on educational research and $130 million on the Social, Behavioral and Economic Sciences (within National Science Foundation). "Clinton's Fiscal-1999 Budget Plan for Higher Education and Science," *Chronicle of Higher Education*, 13 February 1998, A40–A41. Of the roughly 150,000 faculty members in areas related to the social sciences, the *Chronicle* says, a quarter report that they spend a quarter of their time on research, which with an average faculty salary of $50,000 represents nearly a $2 billion public investment in research.

16. Fritz Machlup, who coined the phrase "knowledge industry" nearly four decades ago, warns that "most economists have long since abandoned as hopeless and irrelevant the aim of measuring the total utility or the total benefits obtained from the existence, availability, or consumption of a class of good or service." "Uses, Value, and Benefits of Knowledge," *Knowledge: Creation, Diffusion, Utilization* 1, no. 1 (1979): 77.

17. A further economic factor: most research grants already include a budgetary item (10–15 percent) to cover the dissemination of results, which usually refers to going to a conference to present a paper on the study. A portion of that could go to Automata Data to ensure access for public and practitioner. Also, the fiscal estimate for Information Infrastructure Grants is $20 million for 1998.

18. International Coalition of Library Consortia, "Statement of Current Perspective and Preferred Practices for the Selection and Purchase of Electronic Information," March 1998, http://www.library.yale.edu/consortia/statement.html.

Acknowledgments

If ever a book was a spinoff of collaboration and friendship, this one is indebted to, and thus dedicated to, Vivian Forssman, who in our working together through Knowledge Architecture, Inc. introduced me to the corporate side of what can be done well for a living. This book has also drawn in no small measure on Jennifer Hoffman's talents at Seattle University and Lon Dubinsky's far-reaching wisdom. Parts of the manuscript also benefited from readings by David Coulter, Kieran Egan, Gaalen Erickson, Ricki Goldman-Segall, Ranjini Mendis, Bonnie Norton, and David Sackett, and Avner Segall. Evan P. Young has skillfully copyedited the text, Peggy Swager has carefully crafted the index, and I continue to be well served by Micah Kleit's thoughtful and encouraging editorship. I also want to gratefully acknowledge the support of the Boeing Company, sponsor of the Wm. Allen Endowed Chair of Education at Seattle University, where I spent a stimulating and engaging year with the School of Education while working on this book, as well as the support of the Tele-Learning National Centres of Excellence program of the National Scientific and Engineering Council of Canada.

Index